BUILDING A BEAUTIFUL, INEXPENSIVE STONE HOUSE

CHRIS PROULX

Llumina Press

Requests for permission to make copies of any part of this work should be mailed to Permissions Department, Llumina Press, PO Box 772246, Coral Springs, FL 33077-2246

ISBN: 1-59526-020-X

Printed in the United States of America by Llumina Press

Library of Congress Control Number: 2005907545

DEDICATION

To the good people of Afghanistan and Iraq; we hope that you all have safe, peaceful homes very soon.

And to Trey, Mike, Page and Fishman; so long and thanks for all the Phish.

Did he doubt or did he try?
Answers aplenty in the bye and bye.
Talk about your plenty, talk about your ills,
One man gathers what another man spills.
-Grateful Dead

FOREWORD

With this method of stone house building, even a short, skinny couple such as my wife and I could build fast enough to ultimately move into our new home in just under six months from the date of the excavation to our "shell" being completed. The term "slip forming" isn't like a Tim Wakefield knuckleball; it's straightforward enough. The wood forms are used to form the cement and stone and, when dry, are pried off and slipped up to the next level. This way, the forms are reused until the walls reach the desired height. This method of building turned out to be most economical: we built our own forms, reused them over and again, and the stones were free! It is also efficient, taking approximately half the time it would take to hand-lay stone walls in the traditional way. Therefore, it is especially well-suited for those dealing with short building seasons and small budgets.

The most exciting part of slip form building, we both agreed, was seeing how our walls looked after prying off our forms. On our first try, the wall was as straight as any you'd see around, sturdy, and impressive. Making the first wall as straight as humanly possible involved what I like to call "creative dialogue" between the building partners. And, if someone were lurking in the surrounding thicket with, perhaps, a tape recorder, they could have amassed enough vile language and human hostility so as to rival the entire

Nixon Library of tapes. We quickly discovered that the most strenuous part of building our home this way was agreeing (and prompting Annette to watch her language).

"Oww! That freaking hurt! Damn straight, you'll get the Bactine!"

So, we devised a clever plan by which I would work full time on the weekends, and Annette would work full time during the week, and presto! We nearly eliminated that whole ugly "agreeing" part and worked, mostly solo, at the house on our days off.

I use this charming marital anecdote to further illustrate the feasibility of slip form building your own stone house. I must now also mention the herniated disc in the lumbar portion of my back (which existed prior to the house project). Our combined physical weight was probably less than that of a full-grown Newfoundland hound; I had been given medical advice contrary to what building a stone house requires, and, we worked mostly alone. Facts, fortunately, are as rigid and lasting as the house we built, and it would be tough to argue with the fact that the damn house is built. And, two people who might not strike you as stone house builders at first, second, or any other glance were able to pull it off.

I should also now add that I personally had to overcome nightly volleys of criticism and mental cruelty from my partner, enough to. . . .

"OWW! Will you put down that damn hot poker? Back on the woodstove please? And leave the Bactine with me."

I'm not saying that anyone can build their own stone house, but it would be highly unlikely to find a less apt looking pair than Annette and myself. I must also now say that I wasn't exactly truthful about the mental cruelty and other stuff, but the poker is still very much a problem. We've been to interventions, support groups, watched TV Christian evangelists after many margaritas (this being the only way to accomplish such a distasteful activity) but still, the poker stays. All I can say at this point in our lives is watch out for "the revenge of the mud-throwing maniac" in chapter three, and take assurance in the knowledge that your physical abilities to build a stone house of your own are most likely better than ours.

Chris Proulx, Winter 2004

CHAPTER ONE

PLANNING ON SITE AND SIZE OF HOUSE

When deciding on how to build our home, there were several reasons for choosing stone as a building medium that were pretty obvious. The stones were already on our property, having been delivered as "bank run" gravel the year earlier to make our driveway. Stone is abundant in our area, it lasts longer than wood (or we will, for that matter), and if properly insulated it retains heat far better than wood could ever hope to. The issue of heat retention was perhaps the most important for us, living in Maine and experiencing a winter such as 2003 with low temperatures of 20° below, or colder, for days. I know that I sound like a rich, whiny teenager to the hearty folks in northern North Dakota and Minnesota, but 20° below is still a pretty harsh reality. A thick, insulated stone and concrete house that was also cost effective just made sense to us.

If you have purchased property to build on or previously owned the land, having a stone wall nearby could be a great source of building materials. If you don' t think your property has enough stones, then locate the nearest sand and gravel company and ask for bank-run gravel delivered to your site. Bank-run is a mix of all sizes of stones and comes fairly cheap (we paid $60 per truck load or 12 cubic yards). Unless you have serious transporting equipment, don't try to transport too much stone on your own; this gets extremely heavy and really becomes a mammoth waste of time, loading and unloading the stones by hand. For example, I spotted a huge, quarried piece of granite on one of our dog-walking adventures in a wooded area about ¼ of a mile from the road. The piece was perfect for a basement cornerstone but offered a unique problem: Arnold Schwarzenegger in his heyday, you know, on steroids, would have left both of his expensive Austrian gonads on the ground trying to lift it. A normal person would have left it in its peaceful, bucolic setting. I decided to go back every day before work and roll the freaking behemoth about 50yards each trip until I could load it. A beautiful rock, but a moronic waste of time.

If you have a decent video store in your area try to watch a French film called, "Camille Claudel." It's a sad and tragic story of a woman sculptor who is unjustly hidden in the shadows of the French sculptor and egomaniac, Rodin. But what does this have to do with building a stone house? Well, in the film the woman has, as her mother calls it, "the madness of the mud." She becomes completely obsessed with obtaining her sculpting medium. Obsessed to the point where she would fit in better at a snake handler's convention. I found myself thinking only of stones that I could build with.

Everywhere we walked, ignorantly drove, or hiked, stones were a priority. Obtaining stones became an opiate and a behavior modifying activity that didn't end until we had gathered the last 50 or so that we needed. I've been involved with 12-step programs and self-help groups ever since; one day at a time.

The type of soil you are building on is the first determination to be made when building a heavy, stone house. We recommend that you contact your local Soil Conservation Service, a local well-driller, and your city or town hall for property information such as this. Ask these people about your site and what you are doing; mention specifically that you'd like to know if your type of soil could support the weight of such a building, and also take a look at table 1, provided.

If you are in an area with houses nearby, then chances are pretty good that you can install a septic system, well, and be considered for a building permit. A soil scientist can also do a quick site survey for you, to determine soil types and their suitability for building and designing a septic system. In rural Maine, we had only one obstacle standing in the way of our building site. He weighed about 250 pounds, spoke in a nearly unrecognizable dialect and called himself, "the town CEO" (Code Enforcement Officer). Our first conversation involved much head-tilting, facial contortions, and several perusals through my Ancient Gaelic dictionary to finally understand that we may have needed a special permit for our driveway.

The site we decided to build on was the highest point in elevation on our property and the soil we were to dig into for the basement was hard-packed clay with rock ledge beneath. This was perfect for our home, which we calculated to have a gross weight of 625,000 pounds. This included the outside walls, interior loads, chimney and roof. I'll list the simple math formulas soon, which will help you calculate your house load.

We used a compass to find direct or true south; our full plan was to build an attached solar greenhouse (walls made of stone) the entire length of the southern side of our house. Having the greenhouse located on the southern exposure of the house helps to collect as much sun as possible, naturally heating the inside stone wall and part of the house. Even if you don't include the solar greenhouse, ☙something we highly recommend for the free heat, beauty, potential for enjoyment (hot tubs, saunas) as well as getting an early jump on the gardening season, you really should try to face the long wall of your house toward the south, if possible. Stone walls, when exposed to the sun, collect heat during the day and release it when the sun is down, giving us more free heat. If you go the expensive, Saudi-Bush oil route to heat your home, you'll be spending less on oil and therefore polluting less with a solar greenhouse attached.

We also chose our site based on proximity to the garden area. Just outside the solar greenhouse is our organic garden. For the first three years we raised thousands of seedlings in the greenhouse and easily transported them to the garden via the greenhouse. The garden is in the back yard and allows us easy access to fresh vegetables and herbs. This is just another consideration to make when first designing the layout of your home and landscape. In addition to house plans, it is helpful to draw up a comprehensive site plan. This would detail future buildings, access routes, landscaped areas, fields, and your woodlot, if applicable.

When we purchased our land we were particular when considering acreage. Our property had been for sale for some years. It had been recently logged, and swatches of it resembled the side of Mt. St. Helen's after the blast in '80. Trees were ripped up and used to fill in the tire ruts from the heavy trucks, and other areas were covered with dead trees and limbs, piled 5' high in some spots. Therefore, our property was inexpensive and had enough acreage for everything we wanted. A bulldozer cleared the dead trees for our driveway and we cleared the house site. There is plenty of water on the property (one of our requirements), including a beautiful stream which forms the southern property line and a slow-moving wetland which bisects the property. After the culvert in the driveway was installed, two small pools formed on either side and are now homes to many frogs, small fish, a duck couple that return every year, and a visiting Great Blue Heron.

Where we started

We did the actual clearing for the house site with one chainsaw and many large brush fires that provided nightly warmth and entertainment, as well as a good place to relax after working all day. We left plenty of trees on the north side of the house site to block winds coming down from Canada, which have a tendency to be cold, and began laying out the four corner grade stakes to mark the area to be dug.

When you are setting your grade stakes, it is important to make sure your work is square. This means ensuring that your corners are comprised of 90° angles. To do this, set your first grade stake where you would like one corner of your eventual house to rest. It is important to make sure your stakes are plumb (straight up and down, determined with a carpenter's level) or your measurements will not be accurate. From that point, measure out one side of your house and set another grade stake. We tied a string to a small nail set in the center of each grade stake to mark the line. From your second grade stake, again measure out the next dimension of your home and set another grade stake. Again connect these stakes with sturdy string. Once you have your first corner laid out, you can begin checking for square. The simplest way to do this is to set a carpenter's square on the corner and be sure your strings line up with the square. Continue on by going back to your starting point and measuring out another side of your house. Again, connect the stakes with string and check for square. At this point, you have three sides of your house marked out, and two square corners. If you've done this carefully and correctly, the distance between the two stakes which are not yet attached by string should equal the exact desired length of the last side of your house. If not, you will need to recheck your work and fiddle with the placement of your stakes.

When you are fairly confident that your layout is correct and square, the final test is done by using our friend the Pythagorean Theorem (described in detail a little later). Essentially, measure from one stake along your string a distance of three feet and drive in a plumb stake at that point. Next, measure from that same stake along the perpendicular string four feet out, and again drive in a stake. The distance between these two newly-driven stakes should be exactly 5'. If so, congratulations! You are better than the rest of us and have succeeded in forming a square corner. Chances are, mathematically speaking, if you have one square corner then the rest of your layout is square. Better to check all of your corners, however.

Whether you decide on a basement or not, you still need to have the perimeter dug and footings constructed. If you can operate a rental excavator/backhoe, then you can dig your own perimeter if you decide to go without a basement; this will save you some cash. We did this for our greenhouse and garage foundations in later years. If you choose a basement like we did, you will most likely need someone to dig your basement site for you; a hole 28'x32'x5'-deep (plus a little extra for working room) is something best left for the professionals. Your local sand and gravel company should provide this service.

When you design your home try to plan on a conventional square or rectangular shape. This will make attaching your forms much more problem-free. Avoid trying to achieve a medieval castle feel to it, by planning on semi-circle sections, rounded corners, or bay areas. The simpler and more square the corners, the happier you will be when it comes to setting your forms and working quickly. Don't worry, a square or rectangular stone house is still attractive, unique, and pretty damned impressive. I can almost guarantee that truckloads of people of the gender you are trying to attract will start arriving in your driveway when they discover what you've done; if this doesn't actually happen, then you can at least bask in the knowledge that they are admiring you from afar.

We decided that the dimensions of our house would be, as just mentioned, 28'x32', and our walls would stand 16' from the footing to the sill-plate. What we'll discuss next are the calculations for your footing depth and width. The footing is the base of your home, and along with the pier footings, they carry the entire load (or weight) of the house. To calculate the width and depth of the footing, we first need to calculate the overall weight of the house that will rest on it. To do this we needed the:

A).   Total (in square feet) of floor area.

B).   Total (in square feet) of roof area.

C).   Total (in feet) of perimeter.

D).   Total height (in feet) of exterior walls, from footing to sill plate (or top of wall).

We use the figures for the roof area and floor area to calculate the interior weight of the house. We'll use our home dimensions as examples throughout our calculating processes. To simplify:

Gut Weight =	Roof area + Attic floor area + Floor area x 100 pounds per square foot.
Exterior Weight =	Perimeter x Height x Width x 150 (pounds per cubic foot).
Interior Weight =	Weight of interior walls plus ½ all dead and live loads of first, second, and attic floors. (See Table 2)

To get the figure for our gut weight, we found the roof area first. Annette's "math centers" in her brain are actually inhabited by brain cells that perform math calculations. My genetically acquired "math centers" are currently and always have been hangouts for dullards, under-achievers, and some smelly French guy named Pépé who pukes purple wine. So, we'll smartly turn to her in a second for the roof calculations.

We originally decided on having second floor living space with a shed dormer on the south side for more room. To allow for seven-foot ceilings, Annette calculated that the roof ridge needed to be at least 10' 9-1/4" above the sill plate (we'll turn back to this in a moment). This would give us plenty of headroom in the living area and enough room in the attic to load a small floor area with insulation.

To calculate our roof area for the purpose of estimating loading/footing and material needs (Annette here), we turn back to basic algebra. Yes Chris, when your middle school teacher was trying to convince you that there actually was a use for all that crap, this is exactly what he had in mind. Specifically, we will use the Pythagorean Theorem which states that when dealing with right triangles (those with one 90 ° angle); the square of the longest side will be equal to the sum of the squares of the two shorter sides. Simply put,

$A^2 + B^2 = C^2$. This formula is handy whenever you know the length of two sides of a right triangle and want to know the third, as with our roof. This is also used for checking if your work is square, as described earlier. We knew the height of the gable end wall, and the width of the house we planned to build. The length of the rafters, however, did not just jump out at us.

So, we know that A, the height of the gable wall, is 10'9-1/4" (or 10.77'), and that the width of the house was to be 28'. If we bisect the triangle that is the gable end wall to create a right angle, we get 14' for B (1/2 of 28 is 14). All that remains is to figure the sum of the squares of A and B, and then find the square root of your answer to find C, rafter length. 10.77^2 equals 115.99, and 14^2 equals 196. 115.99+196= 311.99. The square root of 311.99 is 17.66. So, our rafter length from the ridge to the sill plate is 17.66', or 17'8". Finally, the formula to find the roof area is length x width x 2 (there are two sides of the roof). Plugging our values into this, we get 17.66 x 32 x 2, or 1130.24 ft².

In our original plans, we estimated rafter length at 17', and so obtained a roof area of 1088 ft². We will use this estimate in the calculations that follow. It would probably be helpful and more accurate to add in the length of your desired overhang at the gable wall and eaves, and add this to your totals before calculating. We were looking for rough estimates at this point, however, and felt confident that we put enough overbuilding into the underpinnings of our house that the few square feet we underestimated made little difference.

To find the floor area, use the length x width of the first and second floors. The first floor had a length of 32' and a width of 28' (32x28) for a total of 896-ft². The second floor had the same area of 896- ft². So, we added: 896-ft² + 896-ft² for a total of 1,792-ft² of floor area. Our attic area was found by completing the same formula, length x width, to obtain 384-ft².

Now we had the roof area and floor areas totaled and could figure out the gut weight of the house.

$$
\begin{array}{ll}
\text{Roof area} & 1,088\text{-ft}^2 \\
+ \quad \text{Floor area} & 1,792\text{-ft}^2 \\
\hline
& 2,880\text{-ft}^2
\end{array}
$$

We took this total and multiplied it by 100-pounds per square foot for a total of 288,000 pounds for our gut weight. In ordinary construction, this is the only calculation that would be made. However, we are building with stone, and this creates extra weight. To compensate for this, we figured in the estimated weight of our exterior walls, which we will now calculate.

Our basement walls stand 8' from the footing to the first floor ledger, where the first floor walls, which are thinner in width, begin. The basement walls are 16" wide, and we know that the perimeter = 120 ft. The perimeter is found by adding the length of all four walls (28 + 28 + 32 +32). Since the first floor walls are a different width than the basement walls we calculated them separately and added that weight to the weight of the basement walls. The basement walls were first calculated in cubic feet by multiplying:

Height x Width x Perimeter, or

8-ft. x 1.33-ft. x 120-ft. = 1,277-ft³.

We got the 1.33 from the 16" width of the wall. 16" = one foot and four inches or one foot and four inches out of twelve, or 1-4/12. We divided the four by twelve and arrived at .33. We then took the 1,277-ft³ and multiplied it by the standard weight for cement and stone which is 150-pounds per cubic foot, or PCF. We multiplied:

$$1,277\text{-ft}^3$$
$$\underline{X \quad 150\text{-pcf}}$$

For a basement wall total of 191,550 pounds. We next calculated the weight for the first floor walls.

The first floor wall is four inches thinner, so we had different numbers to multiply for the width. It looked like this:

$$8\text{-ft. x } 1\text{-ft. x } 120\text{-ft} = 960 \text{ ft}^3.$$

We again multiplied this by the 150 pcf for a total of 144,000 pounds. We then added this to the total for the basement walls:

$$144,000\text{-pounds}$$
$$+ \ \underline{191,550\text{-pounds}}$$
$$\text{For a total of} \quad 335,550\text{-pounds}$$

This total is added to the gut weight of the house:

$$335,000\text{-pounds}$$
$$+ \ \underline{288,000\text{-pounds}}$$

and we get the total 623,550-pounds that will sit on our footing. We rounded this up to 625,000 (better to overbuild and account for more weight than less). With this weight and one more calculation for the Ground Loading Capacity, derived from the chart to be 2,000-pounds per square foot (being absolutely on the safe side), we arrived at our footing width.

Ground loading is expressed in pounds per square foot (PSF) that certain soils can support. The following values are construction industry standards.

Table 1-1 Ground Loading Capacity

SOIL TYPE	LOADING CAPACITY
Bedrock	160,000
Ledge	40,000
Hardpan or Shale	20,000
Compacted Sand or Gravel	16,000
Loose Gravel	12,000
Coarse Dry Sand or Hard Dry Clay	8,000
Fine Dry Sand	6,000
Silty Sand and Clay	4,000
Wet Sand or Firm Clay	4,000
*Soft Clay	2,000

*Some codes set this limit at 1500 PSF and recommend a soil analysis to determine suitability of these soils for building on.

We first took the 625,000-pounds and divided it by our desired ground loading capacity to determine how many square feet of footing we would need. We obtained a total of 312.5-ft², which we then divided by our perimeter of 120' for a total of 2.60. This 2.60 represents 2-feet, 7-½-inches and this is how wide our footing should be. To be on the really safe side, we rounded up to 3' wide footings. We reasoned that the extra cement poured would be cheap enough when considering peace of mind and durability.

Now that we know how wide the footing should be, we need to discuss the pier footings and their dimensions. If you look at page 55 in Chapter Four, you can see the three pier footings running down the center of the basement. These footings will carry different loads than the perimeter footing. Each floor of the house, the attic floor included, and all the interior walls have both "dead" and "live" loads. A glance at the table (1-2) will show how many pounds per square foot we need to account for with each different load on each floor and for all interior walls.

The "dead weight" of the structure includes all building materials and is no more than twenty pounds per square foot. The "live weight" of the structure includes all of the belongings such as furniture, appliances, cabinetry, as well as the external sources of weight such as snow, rain, and forces of wind. The live loads are all forty pounds per square foot, or less, for the roof and attic floor areas.

Pier footings are able to carry about 1/2 of the dead and live weights of the attic and all floors (first and second in our case), as well as the total weight of interior walls.

Table 1-2 Interior Loads

FLOOR OR AREA	LOADS FOR PIER FOOTINGS LIVE LOAD	DEAD LOAD
First Floor	40 PSF*	10 PSF
Second Floor	40 PSF	20 PSF
Attic Floor	20 PSF	20 PSF
Roof	40 PSF	30 PSF
Interior Walls	----	20 PSF

* PSF pounds per square foot

The pier footings will bear 1/2 of the weight of the first and second floors and attic, plus the entire weight of the partitions. When figuring the total weight, our calculations looked like this:

$$\frac{(\text{weight of first floor x 50 PSF})}{2} =$$

$$\frac{(\text{weight of second floor x 60 PSF})}{2} =$$

$$2(\text{weight of interior walls x 20 PSF}) =$$

$$\frac{(\text{weight of attic x 40 PSF})}{2} =$$

And all of these totals were added up for a total weight resting on the piers. Specifically, our numbers looked like this:

$$\frac{(896\text{-ft}^2 \text{ x 50 PSF})}{2} = \quad 22{,}400 \text{ pounds}$$

$$\frac{(896\text{-ft}^2 \text{ x 60 PSF})}{2} = \quad 26{,}880 \text{ pounds}$$

Interior walls 2(896 x 20 PSF) = 35,840 pounds
And attic $\frac{(384\text{-ft}^2 \text{ x 40})}{2}$ = +7,680 pounds
  92,800 pounds

Again, according to our "ground loading" chart, 2,000 pounds was our figure and we divide our total weight by this:

$$\frac{92{,}800}{2{,}000} = 46.4\text{-ft}^2$$

and this tells us the total square footage that our piers would need to be to spread the load out to the desired pounds per square foot.

Table 1-3   Maximum Spans for Girders

GIRDER SIZE	TWO STORY HOUSE	ONE STORY HOUSE
8 X 10	10'	12'
8 X 8	8'	10'
6 X 10	8'	9'
6 X 8	7'	8'
4 X 10	7'	8'
4 X 8	5-½'	6'4"

Before trying to figure the dimensions of the pier footings we need to know how many footings we need in all. To get this number first take a look at the table on girders. This table lists girders, their sizes, and span limits that you need to take into account in order to calculate the number of piers needed. When deciding on the number of piers, the length of your house is taken into account, and the size and length of the girders, hence the distance between your piers are based on this. For example, our house length is 32' from the east to west sides. Looking at the table again, we found that for a two story house, a 6x10 girder has a maximum span of 8'. According to code, our maximum distance between piers should be no larger than this. So, we would have four spans (32/8=4) or girders, using a minimum of 6x10 lumber. This translates to three piers, when you take into account that the sill supports the ends of the outer girders. Our local lumberyard had 8x10 girders at a good price, so we decided again on over-building for more peace of mind.

If you plan a house that is any wider than ours, you will most likely have to plan on having two rows of pier footings. This is due to the fact that your maximum spans between your sill and your girders would most likely not be over fifteen or sixteen feet, unless you plan on using larger lumber than is customary. Again, see the tables on joist and girder spans to help you make your plans.

Now we'll use the 46.4-ft² (the square footage that the piers will need to be), and we divide this by our three pier footings that will support the weight. We found that each pier needed to be 15.46-ft². We rounded this up to 16-ft² which means that each pier will need to be 4'x4', to handle the load. The piers should also be at least 16" deep, like the perimeter footing. I called around to foundation building companies to ask for standard foundation dimensions and was told by more than one that footings and pier footings should be as deep as the basement wall is wide. Our basement wall is 16" wide and we again decided to over-build and make our footing piers 19" deep (as deep as the forms).

And that's it for calculating footing size, number of piers and pier footing dimensions. Quickly finish a few beers, if you haven't wisely done so already, and relax. . . . I'm serious, try to relax because the next thing we'll do is calculate how much cement, sand, and gravel we'll need to fill the footing and piers (a brief activity) then it's time to do some actual building. Since we were on a tight schedule due to weather conditions in Maine, it was from this point until we put the last pieces of roofing on that I worked and behaved more and more like a sled-dog on crank.

Table 1-4 Maximum Spans for Joists

WOOD TYPE	JOIST SIZE	16 INCHES JOIST SPACING	24 INCHES JOIST SPACING
LARCH, SOUTHERN PINE DOUGLASS FIR	2 X 10 2 X 8 2 X 6	16'5" 12'10" 9'9"	13'4" 10'6" 7'11"
PINES (NOT EASTERN OR SOUTHERN), SITKA SPRUCE	2 X 10 2 X 8 2 X 6	14'6" 11'4" 8'7"	11'10" 10'6" 7'
REDWOOD, SOUTHERN AND NORTHERN CEDAR (WHITE),	2 X 10 2 X 8 2 X 6	13' 10'2" 7'9"	10'4" 8'1" 6'2"

CHAPTER TWO

HOW MUCH CEMENT, SAND, AND GRAVEL WILL YOU NEED?

C alculating the amount of cement, sand, and gravel needs can be done quickly using the numbers we already have and knowing approximately what size stones we are using. Our walls are 16" wide in the basement and 12" wide for the first floor and, our stones were generally around ½ the width of the forms. Stones are cheaper than cement and require less processing; having many small stones means more mixing and spending more money on bags of cement. I know I've mentioned this before but buying a truckload or two of bank-run gravel will give you a nice variety of stones to choose from. Stick with us because after calculating how little it will cost for your cement, sand, and gravel as compared to a current estimate to have your home wood-framed by carpenters, (typically over $100 per square foot) you'll be happy that you did.

We first figured out how much cement we needed for the first floor only since our basement walls, footing, pier footings, and basement pad were poured by a cement company. We did it this way due to the time restrictions inherent in building in central Maine, and highly recommend that you do the same. Filling your basement forms by hand-mixing, and pouring by yourself will add weeks, possibly months to your schedule. If you arrange the forms and the cement company just delivers the cement, you can continue working as soon as the cement is dry.

For the first floor walls the formula we use is simple:

$$\frac{(\text{width x perimeter x height}) / 27}{2} = \text{cubic yards}$$

We divide by 27 in the numerator to get the answer in cubic yards, and by two in the denominator because ½ of the space in the forms will be taken up by stones. Our numbers were:

$$\frac{(1' \text{ x } 120' \text{ x } 8') / 27}{2}$$

for a total of 17.77-cubic yards. And, when we mixed our cement we used a (1:3:4) ratio of (cement: sand: gravel). So what we need to do now is divide our total by the amount of parts of cement in the mix. There are eight total parts, (1+3+4) and cement is 1/8 of the mix; so, our total of $17.77y^3$ is divided by 8 for a total of $2.22y^3$ of cement needed for the first floor walls.

How much is that in bags of cement? Well, each bag is a cubic foot of cement and there are approximately 27 bags in a cubic yard of cement. We needed to multiply the $2.22y^3$ by 27 for a grand total of 59.9 bags and we bought 60. In 2000, the bags of cement were $6.99 per bag, so the total dollar amount for cement for the first floor was $419.40. We include a very close approximation of the total cost to build our home as well as individual costs for materials, tools, rental equipment, and other miscellaneous items in the back of the book. I think that even the most aloof of American consumers will notice that the total cost to build our home was tens of thousands of dollars less than driving a new Hummer off the lot.

The dimensions of the pier footings have been calculated and we figured that we needed three piers with the dimensions (4'x4'x19" deep).

When we calculated the amount of cement needed for the three pier footings we use the formula:

$$\frac{(\underline{width \times length \times height})}{27} \times \text{number of piers}$$

So, we needed; $\frac{(\underline{4'x4'x1.58'})}{27} \times 3 = 2.82y^3$ for our piers.

In 2000, one cubic yard of poured cement went for $57, costing us $160.74 for the three piers.

When we calculate the cubic yards of cement needed for the footing, we use the formula:

$$\frac{(\underline{width \times height \times perimeter})}{27}$$

Our footing dimensions were:

$$\frac{(3'x1.58'x120')}{27} = 21.06\text{-}y^3 \text{ total.}$$

Twenty-one yards of cement is a significant amount so the footing was obviously a bit more money but reasonable for foundation work; the total for this was $1,200.42.

The next big cement delivery was for the foundation walls and to calculate the cubic yards needed we plug the dimensions into the same formula as the footing:

$$\frac{(1.33'x8'x120')}{27} = 47.28\text{-}y^3 \text{ total.}$$

Our basement walls needed more than twice the amount delivered for the footing and was our biggest cement expense at $2,694.96.

If you're going to go through the trouble and expense of digging a basement, you should have a basement pad of nice, smooth poured cement. Basement pads don't require very much cement so the expense isn't so bad. The formula for calculating the amount of cement is:

$$\frac{(\text{length x width x depth})}{27}$$

Most pads are poured 4" thick, but the price was so cheap that we ordered enough cement for a 6" thick pad and the numbers looked like:

$$\frac{(32'\text{x}28'\text{x}.5')}{27} = 16.59 - y^3$$

The total cost for the basement pad was $945.63. When we added the amounts for all of the cement deliveries we came up with $5,001.75. This seems like quite a bit of money for people bent on building their own house. We never really thought so because the cheapest estimate that we received from a foundation company was $14,999.

Now you can estimate the cost of concrete, per bag for stone-wall building, and by the cubic yard when you order your cement.

What we did next is figured out how much sand and gravel we would need. I'm not going to waste your time with more calculations when the most logical thing to do is order what you need when you need it. If your house dimensions are anything similar to ours then start with a full truck-load (usually 10 or 12 cubic yards per load) of both sand and gravel. Again, be sure to inform your sand and gravel company what you need this for and they'll deliver screened sand that is just a bit coarser than beach sand but still fun to stick your bare-feet in or sit down in and relax.

When you order gravel, the company will deliver a huge pile of crushed stones that should be 3" or less in size. This pile will be depleted at a slightly quicker rate than the sand if you choose to use a (1:3:4) mixture like we did. I don't recommend sticking any bare parts of your body in this pile, and truthfully, I've sat on more accommodating species of cactus in my travels.

A full load of cement gravel, 12 yards

After calling around for better prices on sand and gravel you can now get a fairly close estimate of costs for the basement and first floor of your home. If you've looked at the costs included in the back, I think you'll notice that the total for the basement and first floor combined is a mere fraction of what we were originally quoted just to have the basement walls built for us. And, this meant no first floor, which is the majority of our home's living area. Basement walls only. So, when you get outrageous quotes from foundation companies, if you even try dealing with them, you can tell them what I did,

"Screw you guys, I'm going to build my own home," and try to sound like Eric Cartman.

CHAPTER THREE

SLIPFORMING METHOD:
BUILDING, ATTACHING FORMS,
AND WORKING WITH REBAR

The last estimates I received to rent foundation forms to build our basement walls were in the neighborhood of $2,000-$3,000 per week! The man on the phone giving me this quote justified this amount by informing me that they could get three to four foundations built in one week with the forms at an exorbitant fee. We had already decided to build our own forms from the beginning, so I am using the dollar amounts as a reference point. Building our own forms and being able to modify their size as needed was the cheapest and most efficient choice for us. Also, if you have minimal carpentry skills, building your wood forms is an excellent way to practice wood-working. And, making some mistakes during the form building is rather cheap when using cheap wood. It's when you're working with expensive, 20' roof rafters or heavy floor joists that you don't want mistakes. If you look at the pictures of our forms, even a non-carpenter could notice that 2x4s are used for the framing. The best 2x4s for the job were also inexpensive.

Rear view of forms, 9 gauge wire and
2 bundles of grade stakes.

Here is a close-up of two forms with the end studs bolted together and the
tops braced with old pieces of 1 x 6's; they have not yet been leveled.

The 2x4s should be planed as opposed to rough, which is usually obtained from lumberyards. The planed 2x4s should be as straight as possible because the forms will be making right angles and need to be connected. Connecting forms with bowed wood can cause gaps that ooze precious cement, thus wasting your money. So, take the time when you buy your 2x4s to check each one. The length should not be over 8' simply because they start to get way too heavy to move around when they're over this length. The 2x4s should therefore be bought in 8' lengths.

Basic Slipform Construction

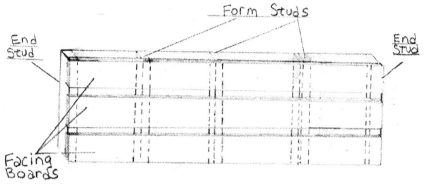

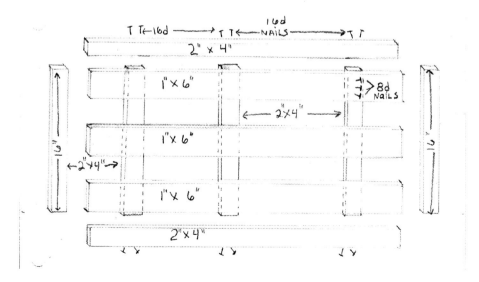

When covering the 2x4 frames we used unplaned or full dimension 1x6 spruce boards. When you arrange the 1x6s with a ½" gap between them, your forms will be 19" wide and you'll find as you go that this is a comfortable height to work with. A 19" wide form by 8' long should be the maximum size of any of your forms; any longer or wider and you reduce maneuverability and increase the chances of dropping them when they're being moved up the wall. The 1x6 facing boards can and probably should be bought in 16' lengths and simply cut in half to make (2)- 8'-foot facers. The unplaned 1x6s were the most economical choice for facing boards and are found cheapest at lumberyards.

When you cut the 2x4s, the long studs for the forms are known as "whalers," and the smaller studs used to connect the whalers are the "form studs." The forms studs should all be cut to 16" lengths because planed 2x4's are actually 1-1/2" and not 2", and when nailed between the two whalers, this adds up to 19" for the desired width of your forms.

When we planned our house, we reasoned that if we made enough forms to be able to fill two sections of wall running the entire perimeter of the house, we'd be able to work almost non-stop just mixing cement and filling forms. We did just this, and found that we could build 120' of stone wall, 19" high in less than one week. We then placed the second set of forms on top of the first section of wall, bolted them together, and were ready to build another 120' wall just as soon as the first section was dry enough. We recommend that when you buy the wood for your forms that you purchase enough to build two complete sets of forms, enough to go around the perimeter twice. Also, it's easier to get razor-straight walls when forms are all aligned at once.

The forms should be uniformly built with the form studs spaced 2' apart, on-center. This allows the form studs to align on both sides where we can wrap our 9-gauge wire around them. Our house plans called for (2) 32' walls and (2) 28' foot walls. For the 32' walls we needed (16) 8' forms and

(12) 8' forms for the 28' wall. We built (30) 8' forms, (8) 4'10" forms, (4) 5'10" forms and (4) 1'10" forms to be able to form-up our entire footing. All of the 8' forms were built uniformly as were the smaller forms. Make the form studs the same distance apart (2') for all of the forms that are of similar size. By doing this the form studs will align when they are facing each other making it easy to wrap our wire around them.

Wire Wrapped Around Form Stud

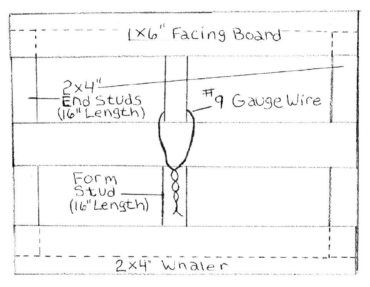

Every form has two form studs to frame the ends; they're called "end studs" and should be 16" long. We drilled the end studs 4" in from both ends with a ½" drill bit. We drilled the first end stud and used it to make copies for the end studs on the other forms so that all drilled holes will align when the forms are bolted together. When the forms are connected we use these holes to slip our bolts through and then we tighten the bolts down. It really is faster to work when these holes are drilled with the same spacing. When the holes line up we can bolt the forms together quicker and easier.

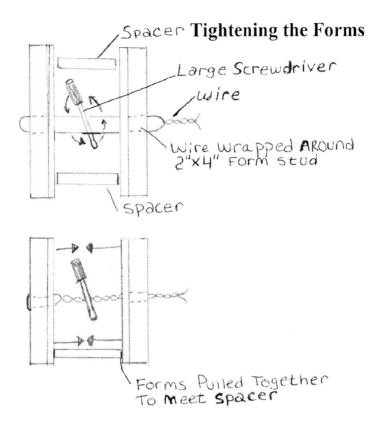

Spacer **Tightening the Forms**

Large Screwdriver

wire

Wire wrapped Around 2"x4" Form stud

spacer

Forms Pulled Together To Meet Spacer

I mentioned that we left a ½" gap between facing boards when building. This enabled us to weave the 9-gauge wire through the ½" space. The wire is wrapped around two form studs facing each other, woven through the gaps in the facing boards, and this is what keeps the forms from dramatically exploding when tons of cement and all the force they bring are poured between them. You can order this wire in 100' rolls and should be cut (bolt cutters are efficient for this) to a size that is twice the width of your forms plus 3-feet, or so. Our footing forms needed to be 3' apart, so I cut the wire into 9' lengths. This was enough to wrap around both form studs, be tied-off at one end and still have enough slack between the forms to insert a large screwdriver between the wires and spin it. This is what tightens our forms together, spinning the screwdriver. Doing this tightens the wires and pulls the two forms together until they're at the correct spacing.

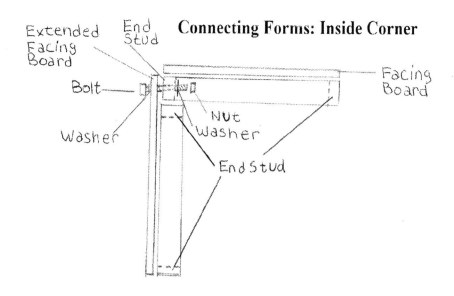

When the forms are at the correct distance apart, brace them over the top with scrap 2x4s or 2x3s to keep them at the correct spacing. We nailed these down with 10d nails, or bigger, if you don't mind the extra crowbar work prying them off again. We don't recommend smaller nails because we're dealing with heavy cement. We cut a scrap 2x4 to a length of 3' and made a copy. The two pieces of 2x4 are used as "spacers" and they're placed horizontally between the forms while we tighten the wires with the screwdriver. When the spacers are held snugly in place between the forms, one at the top and one at the bottom; the forms are then at the correct spacing. When this is done, we pop out the spacers with a hammer and reuse them until they wear down or break.

Connecting the forms together is pretty simple. We bought about 100 or so, 7/16" bolts, 5" long, along with nuts and plenty of washers. Get the cheap ones, not the galvanized hardware since you may need them only for the form building, like we did. When working on the footing forms that have been designated for corners, we cut the facing boards 4" longer than the end stud and connected the corner forms using 4" bolts (completely threaded). We placed washers on both sides of the bolts so the hex-nut ends didn't dig into the wood when we tightened them up. The bolts were tightened, but not so much as to bend the washers. The bolts should be connected tightly using a box wrench on the nut and a ratchet and socket on the bolt.

When the forms were arranged and connected together, we then began working with rebar. Rebar is what helps strengthen concrete. It can be bought in ½" thickness and up to lengths of 20'. According to footing standards, we placed 3-concentric rectangles of rebar propped up on stones (2" minimum off of the ground). We did this before bracing the tops and wiring the forms tight because the braces and wires would simply be in the way.

Bolting Forms Together

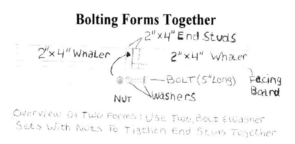

Overview Of Two Forms: Use Two Bolt & Washer Sets With Nuts To Tighten End Studs Together

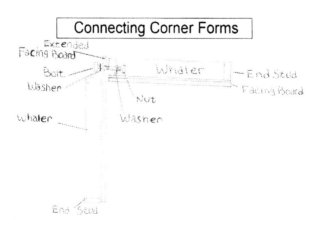

Connecting Corner Forms

Here is the rebar tied together at the ends with
16 gauge wire and propped on stones.

We tied the lengths of rebar together with 14 or 16-gauge wire. We cut the wire to approximately 2' lengths and wrapped it tightly around the ends of the rebar to connect them. Overlap the ends of the rebar to be connected by 1' or so. If you see the photo with the corner shot, you'll notice the rebar is bent at a 90° angle. This is done easily with a 3' piece of hollow steel pipe. Slip the pipe over the end of the rebar and bend the rebar by propping one end against a steady object such as a tree trunk or anything that won't budge. Pull the pipe and step on the rebar in the area that needs to be bent. Doing it this way, the rebar is bent without extreme effort.

Cutting rebar is done with a circular saw and diamond composite blades. Don't try to use bolt cutters or hacksaws to cut rebar; you'll waste plenty of time and physical energy. When we reinforced the pier footings, I bent the rebar into 90°, enough to be able to form one 3x3 square and one 2x2 square.

They fit inside each other and these were placed in the forms for the pier footings. They were then placed on top of stones, keeping them off the ground.

Footing forms with braces, wires, rebar and basement drain pipe

If you look at the photo, you'll notice a 4" section of P.V.C. pipe running through the forms. This is our basement drain pipe. If you build in a wet area a basement drain is helpful if you should encounter water problems. It is also helpful if you plan on a root cellar or ever have a plumbing problem. The pipe was placed flush with the bottom of the footing, via a hole cut into the footing form for that purpose. It should protrude at least 1' from each of the forms, so that you can easily add more pipe to it when you are ready. It should be placed according to where the excavation crew deems to be the best place, or closest to a hill on your property so that a trench can be dug out to provide positive drainage. You'll also notice in the photo that the rebar is laid on top of the pipe, the wood braces are cut, and the lengths of wire are cut and ready to be woven through the forms. We counted how many braces and lengths of wire were needed for the entire footing and cut them all before bracing or wiring any of the forms. I found that it was quicker to cut them in assembly-line fashion than to run back to the large coil of wire, or to the saw for individual pieces.

After the horizontal rebar had all been tied together and propped up in place, it was time to arrange the forms in a straight line around the perimeter (both inside forms and out). The forms were loosely bolted together at this point. To line up the forms as accurately as possible, we drove two small nails into the tops of the forms in each corner. We nailed them into the middle of the facing boards and tied a string to the nails. The string was long enough to stretch corner to corner above the top of the forms. When the string is taut, you can easily see where your forms are not in alignment. We placed a large carpenter's square on top of the corner braces just below the strings and made the strings fall into line with the square. With a nudge or the blow of a hammer this way or that, the forms are brought into line and then the bolts are tightened. The forms were now straight all around and needed to be wired together and braced over the top.

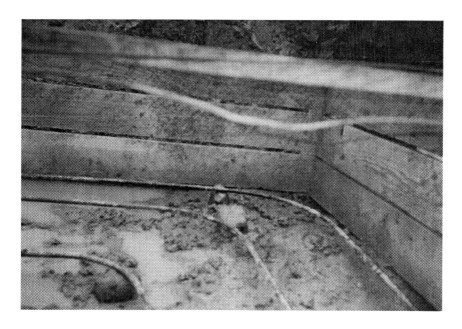

Inside corner of the footing forms with 3 rows of rebar.
Notice gaps Between facing boards for wires.

We have read of others using batter boards, plumb lines, and chalk lines to get their forms to line up and it makes some sense. Batter boards are essentially like our grade stakes, described earlier, that marked the lines of our building for the excavator. The difference is that batter boards are set up further back from the building site; far enough back so that they are not in the way of the excavator or the builders, and are a semi-permanent fixture/reference point on the building site. A batter board is usually made of a 1x4 or 1x6 board (use scrap lumber), supported by stakes or 2x4's driven into the soil which are then braced to be plumb and level. Nails are driven into the top of the 1x6 to mark the lines of the inner and outer footing and basement walls. There are four such batter boards placed, one for each wall.

When the strings are all taut board to board, and then accurately mark where your footing edges should be. You can then transfer these lines from the batter boards to the ground giving you the location for your footing. To do this you simply tie two pieces of string to each end of the batter board marking the location of the footing corners. To the other end tie a couple of washers for a plumb bob and drop it to the ground. The two points on the ground represent the footing corners and if you pound grade stakes at these points and tie a string between them, you have a straight line to line up the footing forms. As usual, we found more "creative" ways to go about our work.

Inside corner showing extended facing board bolted
through end stud and braced on the top

Wiring the forms together came next. When cutting the 9 gauge wire, cut one piece that is long enough to weave through the forms, leaving enough slack to be able to twist the wire tightly around the form stud. We used this first piece, once we checked it for fit, as a model to cut the rest. When you weave the wire through the ½" gap between the facing boards, slip it between the bottom and middle facing boards and over to the opposing form. The wire then goes through the gap between the bottom and middle boards of the opposing form and wrapped around the form stud. You should then twist the ends of the wire together around the form stud, loosely at first because they will be tightened later. We placed wires between the gap of the top two facing boards, same as the bottom and were ready for top braces.

We wired each 8' form up with at least three wires; one around each end stud and one around the middle form stud. Others may opt to wire each stud, but we found that wiring three studs in each form was more than adequate. Even with the impact of the heavy cement being dropped from the truck, the forms did not budge, and our footing came out perfectly. Before you decide to wire up every form stud, consider the fact that the wires often get in the way whether you are dragging cement, placing stones, or setting in rebar.

With the forms wired up, it was time to tighten them to our desired width. We placed our 3' spacers between the forms; one placed near the bottom and one at the top, and twisted the wire between the forms until the forms came into contact with the spacers. At this point the forms were at the desired 3' width from top to bottom. We then went around the entire footing and tightened the wires just so.

The same wiring scheme is used when setting up the pier footings. Cut these wires much longer than for the regular footing or wall forms. Crisscross the wires inside the forms and tighten snugly to the correct spacing, as above. Brace the tops with 2x4s, as described below and bolt all the corners together.

You are now ready to brace the tops of your forms. Leave the spacers between the forms when bracing the top to maintain the correct spacing. We used top braces across the ends of the forms and in the middle, using three braces per 8' form. These braces eliminate the need to wire the tops of the forms. The forms were now exactly 3' wide and held very tightly together.

One more task at this point is checking your forms for plumb and level. These are both done with a carpenter's level. To check for plumb, the level is placed vertically along the inside of each form, against the facing boards, as well as along the outside, against the form studs. Checking the forms for plumb is absolutely imperative if you do not desire that your finished creation resembling the Leaning Tower of Pisa. A tiny bit off plumb at the bottom can set your entire project off. Of course, if you do make a mistake and detect it early you can correct for it at the next course, but it is better to not err to begin with.

If a form was found to be slightly off plumb, this was corrected with 2x4 braces. Bracing was accomplished by pushing against the form with one end of a 2x4 and propping the other end against a grade stake driven into the ground. Once the form or wall was plumb, we lightly nailed the 2x4 into the form. We did check our walls at each level for plumb, and were rewarded accordingly with walls that were, well, plumb.

Another quick note here about plumb and lumber. We often came across situations where the forms were plumb, but because the facing boards were of uneven thickness, they did not register as plumb. This is the reason for checking both the inside and the outside of the forms. For a compulsive perfectionist like myself (Annette speaking here), this was gloriously agonizing. For Chris, watching me pull my hair out over 1/32 of an inch here or a micron there was just plain agonizing. Be assured, as I wasn't, that this normal amount of variability does not mean that your entire project is doomed to failure and you'll spend the winter living in a van down by the river. As long as you are careful about checking for plumb and level at each course, your project will come out just fine.

Checking for level is next. This is done easily by placing your level (the longer the level the better) on top of each form and, if needed, shimming here and there underneath to make sure your course is absolutely level. Another check that is pretty helpful and informative is to check your opposing walls for level using a water level. A water level is a clear plastic hose that can be found at just about any hardware store and comes with basic but comprehensive instructions on its use. We did try one of the newer, electronic leveling tools but found it to be of limited use. Whether this was a fault of the tool or the operator's isn't clear.

Shows vertical rebar every four feet, location of braces, And grade stakes
pounded in against the forms, they stick Up slanting inwards

I talked about laying horizontal rebar in the bottom of the footing, but now we need to talk about vertical rebar. If you look at the photo and the illustration on page 40, you'll see the vertical rebar sticking up out of the cured concrete footing. This rebar needs to be spaced at 4' on center and should be set running down the center of the forms. This vertical rebar will run right through to the top of your cement and stone walls, which, together with the horizontal rebar (spaced apart at 24" on center), forms a web of steel that protects your home from the ravages of time and weather. This is an important consideration when building with stone, especially if you live in an earthquake-prone area, and the state of Maine is one area where using more is better. The rebar (vertical and horizontal) is all tied in together with a fine, 14 gauge wire, and should overlap by a foot at all joints.

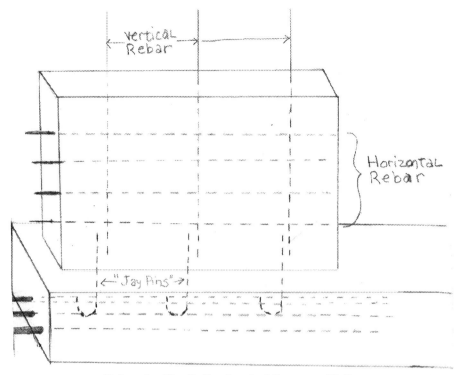

Rebar, Jay Pins In Footing And Basement Walls

If the cement moves your rebar when it is poured, you'll have time to reset and straighten them out before the concrete sets. To set the rebar in a strait row, use a string and two nails pounded into the tops of the forms at either end (one corner to the next). Tie some string to the nails and use this as a guide to line up your rebar.

When we ordered the rebar we first figured how much we'd need for the footing, pier footings, and walls. We also ordered some extra lengths of rebar for "jay pins" or "footing keys" (see illustration on previous page). These are set in the drying concrete to keep the basement walls from sliding out of position. When cutting rebar for drift pins place the rebar in a vice and, using the circular saw and diamond composite, metal cutting blades, cut the rebar into 2-foot lengths. After cutting (30) 2' lengths of rebar, enough to set one drift pin every 4 feet down the center of the footing (in line with the vertical rebar), I placed them one by one in the vice. Buy a wide, heavy vice if you don't already have one. I found a sturdy, old model at a yard sale for a very good price.

Here is a jay pin and a roll of 16 gauge wire for tying rebar together, bolt cutters for the 9 gauge wire.

The drift pins need to resemble a basic fish-hook, without the lip-piercing pointy end, of course. To do this, grip the 2' lengths of rebar about half-way, vertically, in the vice and tighten securely. Slip the steel pipe (about 4" down) around the end pointing upward, and pull down until it resembles a hook. After bending the drift pins, we tossed them in a pile since we wouldn't need them until the concrete was poured. But I will quickly mention how we set them. We took the drift pins and stuck the hook end into the drying concrete, leaving about 10" to 1' above the surface. Don't wait until the concrete is too hard, but don't set them when the concrete is too wet to support them either. After smoothing the surface of the concrete with a trowel, the time that had lapsed seemed perfect to set the drift pins. They sank in with not too much effort, and we smoothed the concrete over again around the pins with the trowel.

Footing Dimensions: 29' 10" x 33' 10"

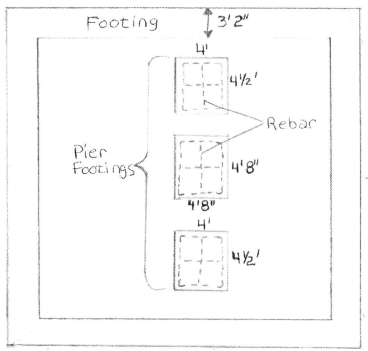

There was one more thing we needed to do before the concrete was poured. Flush against the bottoms of the forms we pounded some 3' grade-stakes every 4' or so. This was extra support for the forms and prevented them from moving outward.

When setting the grade-stakes, we took a heavy hammer, placed the stake against the bottom (2x4) and pounded them down, making certain they were snug. When pounding them in we went about 1-½' into the ground and placed them next to the inside and outside forms.

Now we were ready to call for the cement delivery. If you've looked at the pictures you may have noticed that our working conditions were pretty sloppy. It had rained for 2 days before we started work on the footing and slogging around in shin-deep mud was about as much fun as a cheap beer hangover. When stepping in the gloppy stuff if surrounds and morphs into your boots until they're either sucked off, or they weigh five more pounds with each step. It was around this time that the mud, which I'd sworn off as my enemy, had momentarily become a valued friend, asset, and projectile. You see, dear reader, that the poor weather and the barrage of complaints from my partner had left me with no options but to counter attack with big gloopy mud balls when she least expected it. Notice the terror in her eyes, the hysterical look of fear and panic as I snuck up on her?

Annette being ambushed by the demented mud monster

No, neither did I and the mud ball counter-insurgency went horribly wrong.

After my brief visit to the emergency room, we were ready for the cement delivery, and the slack-jawed staring followed by the nudge-nudge, wink-wink, and giggle responses from the cement guys. Go ahead, try and tell these hairy, knuckle draggers what you're up to without receiving a good ol' toothless grin.

"You're building a what?"

"Why the hell is the footing so wide?"

"Hey, where are my potato chips?" This was a small sample of the hired goon questioning we had to tolerate, and most likely you will too until your stone walls are completed.

CHAPTER FOUR

BUILDING THE BASEMENT WALLS AND PAD

When the cement had dried for the footing, about 4days in all, the forms needed to be pried off. I won't fudge with you about this part of building the house. Prying the footing forms off can be frustrating. We first unbolted all the connected forms, snipped the wires tied around the studs leaving them in the walls, and put the bolts and other hardware in a large can to use them again. Then we slipped crowbars between the cement and the forms and began prying; some were badly stuck and required new, creative swearing. I found that vulgar names to human body parts linked with inappropriate action verbs worked wonders on the forms.

Footing is drying and forms are built for the basement walls

About 4 of the 8' forms needed repair after prying them from the footing. The outer forms were removed and we were ready to set them on the footing to begin building the basement walls. Compared to working on the footing, the basement walls are much easier to set up and remove, simply because we have more room to work. We weren't as closed-in by the excavation walls and we had the footing to stand on instead of the mud.

Before setting the forms up on the footing, we cleaned the broken pieces of cement and other debris off of the surface. Some of the forms needed to be cut down to fit the smaller perimeter of the basement walls. When cutting the forms we used a circular saw and cut right through the whalers and facing boards to get the correct length. Then we took the end stud off of the section that was just cut and re-nailed this into the forms, as the new end stud. Again, we connected enough forms to make a complete wall section spanning the whole perimeter of the footing, set on top.

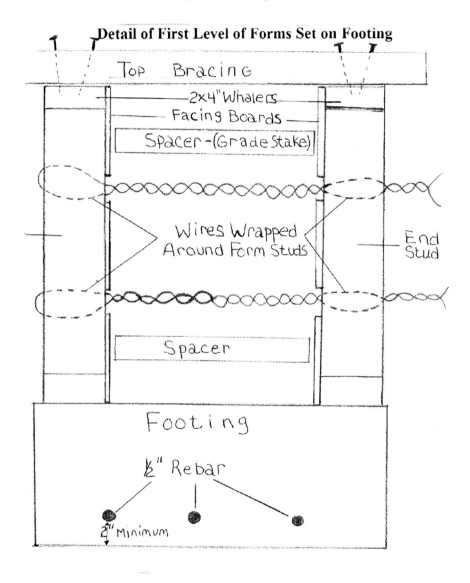

Detail of First Level of Forms Set on Footing

Top Bracing

2x4" Whalers

Facing Boards

Spacer - (Grade Stake)

Wires Wrapped Around Form Studs

End Stud

Spacer

Footing

½" Rebar

2" Minimum

Fourth layer of basement wall being poured,
Note 2x4 braces propped against third layer to
keep from shifting when cement is poured.
We're pulling the cement here.

When setting the basement wall forms on the footing, we centered them and used a chalk-line snapped on the footing as a guide. We basically arranged a smaller rectangle on the larger rectangular footing. Our basement walls are 16" wide so we needed to cut new spacers to that same length. The forms were then wired, and horizontal rebar was placed on top of the wires setting them off the surface of the footing. We used one row of #4 rebar at 32" on center with an extra piece in the corners for extra reinforcement. The rebar was then wired to the 9-guage wires, which helps to keep them in place when the cement is poured. The vertical rebar sticking up from the footing continued through the basement walls and I didn't need to connect more vertical rebar until the 5th level of basement wall was poured.

Now that we had our forms all arranged and braced, they needed exterior bracing to keep them from shifting when the cement was poured. To brace the interior set of forms, we propped one end of an (8') 2x4 against them like we did with the footing, then positioned the other end against grade stakes pounded into the ground. The exterior set of forms were braced by using 2x4's cut to length and we wedged them between the forms and excavation walls. This kept the basement wall forms from moving laterally. The first pour for the basement walls is especially crucial for the correct alignment of the rest of the wall and the rest of the house.

Within one day of work the forms were ready. The delivery came the day after and we had our first section of basement wall finished. When you have a cement delivery, you really should try to ask one or two friends for help "pulling" the cement. Cement companies deliver cement and they don't provide labor to move the cement; you need to do this. Due to the nature of the medium, it is best to have the forms completely filled as quickly as you and your help can pull the cement around the forms. The cement will sit where it is poured and needs to be moved by shovel. And, since cement doesn't like being moved very much, having access to all areas of the forms with the cement chute is extremely helpful. Cement shouldn't be pulled more than a few feet so try to have the work area vacant for the cement truck to move around easily.

I was able to move the cement chute to where we needed it,
this eliminates extra pulling. Notice septic pipe in corner,
and 2 x 4's propped against lower set of forms.
My dog "Surly" supervising the project.

If you can find a patient delivery person, and they're as easy to find as a keg of beer in a mosque, then they'll be willing to work with you. When our cement was being poured we asked the delivery guy to position the truck and the cement chute (the guy let me move the chute to wherever I wanted it) so as to eliminate too much pulling. As you can see from the photos, the cement is guided through the forms much like oppositionally defiant water, because it will resist your guidance if possible. The photos show three sections of 19" wall already poured and we're working on the fourth.

Here we are pulling the cement to level it off,
notice the pier footing just behind my shovel.

The forms are very strong due to the top braces and
being bolted into the section of forms beneath them. When
this section was dry enough we unbolted the bottom set of
forms and slipped them directly on top of the set we were
working on. We bolted them together again, wired, braced
them and were ready to build the next 19" section of
basement wall.

Filling a pier footing, notice 2 x 4's supporting the inside
and outside, lower section of forms held in place with
with grade stakes.

Third and fourth sections of forms, septic drain pipe (4" pvc), vertical rebar
and top braces. Pad has been poured here, there's a lolly column
In the bottom right corner: also, notice Jim's truck. Jim was on site to
distract Chris with beer, as well as to help and take photos.

We wanted at least (2), 19" sections of wall poured before we worked on the pad; the first section of basement wall acts as a set of forms for the pad, enclosing the cement and forming it. Beneath the pad is approximately 20" of bank run gravel spread evenly.

The pier footings have dried and the forms removed. There is gravel piled in the lower part of photo, this will be spread over the piers.

We first took measurements of 20" from the ground going up the basement walls in each corner and one in the center of the walls. Then we snapped chalk lines to be our guide as to how high we needed the gravel to be. This much gravel would also cover the pier footings by 1", so we made certain of their location in our notes. The columns will be placed on the pier footings, and we needed to take measurements from the walls to the piers to note all of their distances. When it was time for us to set up our lolly columns we referred to the notes and location of the piers.

The photo shows the basement drain and the P.V.C pipe in the far right corner. This pipe should be extended 24" or more vertically, so it's not buried by the gravel or the cement that will be poured around it.

Here the gravel's been spread, the basement drain is in the
right corner, the vapor barrier is rolled out on the gravel
and the 4 inch wire mesh over that. Temporary stones on the
end to flatten it

I think we needed 20 or so yards of gravel dumped into the basement site and we spread it with shovels. You can get fairly accurate with a good set of chalk lines on the walls and a 7-10' carpenter's level. Simply lay the level on an area of gravel that you think is close to level and check it. If not level, spread some more until the gravel is level. With 1" of the pier footings covered with gravel, we next needed to spread a vapor barrier.

The vapor barrier is spread completely covering the gravel.
I placed temporary stones on the end due to wind.

Vapor barriers are thick sheets of plastic that can be rolled out easily and cut to the right size with a box cutter. They stop any moisture from reaching the underside of the cement which could cause eventual cracking and deterioration of the pad. They're available at most hardware stores and usually come in different sizes. A hole for the basement drain-pipe was carefully cut out in the vapor barrier and we were ready for the wire mesh reinforcement.

Two sections of wall poured, third set of forms attached, the vapor
barrier is rolled out and the basement drain pipe is high enough to
avoid being covered over by the cement.

When ordering this, ask for 4" wire mesh reinforcement
for basement pads and the service reps should know exactly
what you're asking for. As you can see, the mesh is rolled out
on top of the vapor barrier and I used stones to keep the ends
from rolling back and upward, or from bulging along the
edge. The larger stones were removed when the cement was
poured and the weight of the cement with the smaller stones
still on the ends was enough to keep them down. The wire-
mesh takes very little time to roll out, but needs to be
trimmed if it doesn't fit exactly. We used tin-snips to cut the
mesh to fit within the basement walls and were ready to call
for the next cement delivery.

Pouring the basement pad is much easier than pouring
into the forms. The cement was moist when poured and I
guided the cement chute to all four corners and the center
of the basement. To get the cement up to 6" evenly, we again
had chalk lines on the basement walls as our guides. We

smoothed the surface of the pad with the backs of our large shovels and a 1' wide by 3' long piece of plywood with 2x4 blocks nailed to one side for hand grips. I used this to smooth over more surface area quicker, before the cement began to set.

I'll quickly summarize the construction of the basement pad. We spread gravel at least 8" deep throughout the basement area. Then we rolled out a thick, plastic vapor barrier over the gravel and cut a hole for the basement drain. Then, we spread out the 4" square, wire mesh over the vapor barrier, and snipped the ends so that the wires would not stick upward through the cement. We then marked the basement walls with chalk lines to indicate how deep the cement pad needs to be poured. A simply made, wide plywood trowel was used to smooth over a large area before the cement began to set and we smoothed our footprints before jumping out of the basement.

We were lucky enough to have beautiful weather when we had the pad poured making the job even more enjoyable. Having a fairly smooth, clean surface to place our tools on was another plus. Amidst the pleasant weather though, the main concern when pouring the basement pad is moving fast enough when smoothing the surface. Unless you're smoothing over a small area one person should not attempt this alone. With two people smoothing the pad we needed to work like kids in a GAP factory. If you have any drinking buddies that can keep it together for an hour or two in the morning, our cement was usually delivered in the morning, then try to recruit at least one or two preferably with the brew-shakes, to help out. Some shaky hands with a large wooden trowel in them will mimic the vibrating motion of the expensive cement smoothing machines. Just guide them in the right direction, hang the customary bucket around their neck for potential bouts of nausea and this should set you back just a simple case of cheap beer.

When the cement hardened we marked areas down the center of the pad with a dot of spray paint, where the pier footings were underneath. We had some stone walls to build before we could set our columns on the pier footings, but with the measurements fresh in our notes and minds we didn't regret doing this, afterward. One thing I did regret not doing, though, was cutting the basement drain pipe level with the surface of the pad. We had a beautiful summer rain the night after pouring the pad and we awoke to a basement pool. This was remedied with a hacksaw and push broom, and the pipe was immediately covered with a plastic, mesh drain cap to keep anything from falling in and clogging it.

I forgot to cut the drain pipe, it rained, and here's Annette taking care of it.

It was nice having the pad finished. This was our first living area, sort of, and we didn't have to deal with the cement guys anymore until the next year. It was win-win. I'm all for watching Bush supporters eat greasy, fatty foods and wash it all down with boloney; they're on a highway to heart attack. Hey, one less red vote. But having to see someone crunch through three bags of pork rinds for breakfast is where my stomach draws the line; with vomit.

CHAPTER FIVE

BUILDING EXTERIOR WALLS: BASEMENT WALLS TO SILL PLATE

A preview of the completed, exterior walls with sill plate on top. The forms have been completely removed and are ready to be stored for next year's greenhouse project.

Up to this point in the construction of the house, we had been working entirely on dirt and clay (and, when it rained, 2 plus inches of mud). Having that smooth basement pad to walk on was really sweet. When we were building the stone walls though, we were right back in the clay and mud, and some of this needed to be backfilled. We made calls to find the best price for a small bulldozer to do the backfilling and had a couple of days to wait for the delivery. This was fine since we still had to lay drain tile all along the perimeter of the basement walls (placed on top of the footing and snug against the wall).

Drain tile is 4" P.V.C. pipe with holes for water seepage. We laid these pipes out on top of the footing, covered them with a layer of mesh screen to keep silt out and then shoveled about 2' of gravel on top of them to help with drainage problems. We used bank run gravel to cover the drain tiles simply because it is cheaper to use than the cement gravel, which needs more processing before it's delivered. Now we were ready to close the perilous gap that I had painfully stumbled into more times than I would care to speak of.

Just before the backfilling, this is the last section of basement wall forms: the septic pipe is in place, the corners are bolted through the facing board and the vertical rebar is set.

Backfilling is done usually by a rented machine or a subcontractor. We ended up having our sand and gravel company perform this task for us, and it was done in short order. If you decide you would like to do this job yourself with a rental, try to reserve the machine for the day you think you will need it well in advance. You will often find in the peak of the building season that you need to wait an inconvenient length of time for equipment that wasn't reserved and waiting.

The backfill was leveled off just beneath the last set of basement wall forms, so we could easily pry them off. We arranged this set of forms on top of the previously poured set of forms and again bolted, wired and braced them tightly. This would be our first set of forms filled with stone and cement, as well as the level of the basement wall where we put our basement window frames. Do not repeat this mistake!! We miscalculated and should have put the windows in the next course. We have compensated for this by extra backfill, galvanized steel wells around the windows, and rebar lintels placed over the windows to provide additional support.

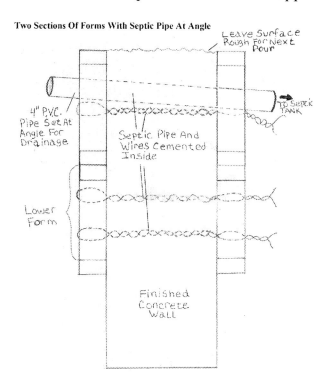

Two Sections Of Forms With Septic Pipe At Angle

Leave Surface Rough For Next Pour

4" P.V.C. Pipe Set At Angle For Drainage

To Septic Tank

Septic Pipe And Wires Cemented Inside

Lower Form

Finished Concrete Wall

Here is a basement window and a few sections of stone
wall built. The lower forms were removed and are ready
to be moved on top of those in place

Basement windows are absolutely necessary; like intolerance to the G.O.P. The windows allow for ventilation in the summer months. Ventilation eliminates moisture build-up on basement walls and wood, which leads to hazardous mold and wood decay--two things I would want in my basement about as much as uh, well, an intolerant G.O.P. boy. I'm sorry. I'm being a bit harsh. I probably shouldn't speak so ill of mold and wood decay. We actually get antibiotics from mold and decayed wood makes great mulch. I'll try not to do that again.

The first thing we needed to know when framing our basement windows was the sizes that they come in. We called around and asked for the outer dimensions of the windows and with this we could build the proper size window frames. The frames were made from 2x12x8' planed boards. We cut them, as shown in the photo, and nailed them together using 16d nails. When the frames were done we nailed 10d nails to the outside of the frames so they were sticking out about 1-½" or so (the photo shows the nails in the door frame). This keeps the frames from shifting in the cement and adds a surface that cement can easily grab onto, since it tends to shrink back a bit from the frame as it dries. Having the nails is like having an extension of surface area around the frames. We nailed them down around the outsides of the frames, top, sides and bottom.

Our forms at this point of construction were 16" wide and the window frames were only 12" wide. We set the window frames toward the interior wall side of the forms and cut 6" pieces out of scrap 2x4's to extend the window frame. The scrap pieces were used to build another smaller frame that would increase the width of the frames to 16" wide. Most residential basement walls are not 16" wide and finding a 2x16 planed board would be difficult and costly. This width may also compromise the strength of the window frame.

The completed window frame, without window inserts, needed to be water-sealed before setting it into the cement. There's an intelligent paint company included in the back. They make and sell products that won't do things like kill you, your pets, and children with toxic additives. Most treated woods, at the time of writing this, are soaked in substances containing arsenic that release toxic vapors, and leach into soils. As a species, I'd say that we've boldly destroyed and polluted as much of the planet as we selfishly could have, and adding extra toxins into the soil around your home is about as dumb as a Baptist think-tank.

If you purchase toxic-free sealers, then apply liberally over the exterior sides and use 2-3 coats on the interior sides. After this, we dropped the frames into the forms. There was a layer of rebar in the way, and I cut this back so it would be up against the frames. Then the frames were set on top of the previously poured layer of concrete, in its planned location.

After setting the basement windows in place, we set two layers of ½" rebar over each frame, and tied this into the existing network of rebar. These serve to support the weight of the stone walls above them. Four basement windows are recommended for proper ventilation and should be set in opposing walls. They should also be set up with flashing or some sort of a draft barrier, described shortly.

This is the east side with two basement windows. We placed
two more on the west side, same distances apart. The door
Frame is also in the wall.

When building the door frames, we again used 2x10's and notched the ends before nailing them together. The photo shows the door frame with braces, notch in the top corner, nails in the sides and a strip of aluminum flashing stapled around the outsides. The flashing was stapled flush with the inside edge of the frame and extending 2" over the outside edge. This is necessary around all of the sides of all frames because it prevents an air space (think draft) between the frame and the cement when it dries. We then set in the door frames in the east, west and south sides of the house. A carpenter's level is helpful when setting in your frames. Place it on top of the frame to be sure your door openings are level. If they're off by a bit, simply add a bit of mixed cement underneath the left or right side until it is level.

Here is a door frame. Notice the notch cut in the top and side boards, the flashing across the front, the 2 x 4 bracing and nails pounded halfway into the boards.

The braces are very helpful when making the door frames perfectly square. We placed a large carpenter's square in the corner of the frame and adjusted the frame until it conformed to the metal square. When the top board and side board made a 90° angle, we nailed the diagonal cross-braces down as shown. This kept the corners in their 90° angles, and we did this to each frame.

We placed our basement window frames in the first section of stone wall instead of including them in a poured section. Our plan was for 7' ceilings in the basement and setting the window frames in the next section would have made them slightly inaccessible to the vertically challenged, such as us. If you've noticed the height of the door frame from the ground, it seems high to the average person. We had planned on a wrap-around porch and needed the extra height to build the large deck, one step down from the door entrance. The space beneath the deck could be easily insulated having enough space to work with.

With all the frames built, we put the window frames in place and the door frames aside. It was time to gather the stones for the exterior walls. When the nice looking building stones had all been picked from the driveway, we started gathering more from the huge pile of bank run gravel sitting near the site. Before building any walls, we first amassed a pile of stones that we thought would possibly be enough for the whole project. By doing this, we were able to continue stone-wall building at a quick pace; otherwise we'd have found ourselves running off in search of more stones whenever we ran out.

The kind of stones that should be used when building, depends on type, size, shape and finally, appearance. We found ourselves using more basalt and granite than any other types. Granite has been a staple in New England when building basement walls. The large quarried stones used for basements are not only attractive but extremely durable and efficient as a building medium. The basalt stones were smooth for the most part and also very strong. We split some of the types of stones we were going to use by dropping them on others or taking a sledge hammer to a few of them. The granite and basalt were the toughest to split and would hold up the best.

The size of the stones should depend on a couple of factors. The width of the forms is the first and the weight of the stones the second. They need to fit comfortably into the forms, not take more than 2/3 of the space between the forms and should be easily moved. Heavier stones pose more handling problems and often need two people to set them and hold them while cement is shoveled behind and around. The accumulated effect of using all heavy stones can be physically bothersome as well. You really don't want to be moving your stones around too many times. When we calculated the full weight of all the stones and cement used in our house, the number came to between ½ and 1million pounds. This calculation is based on a one-time weight of the cement and stone, not moving them two, three, sometimes many more times before being placed in the wall. Lifting that much weight in a four-month span can take its toll on even the fittest biped.

When considering the shapes of the stones used, we gathered some for the wall faces and some for the corners. The stones for the wall face that we chose had to have a nice flat face and be at least 4" thick. The flat surface would be placed against the inside of the exterior wall form and would be exposed when the forms are removed.

Cornerstones need to fit comfortably into the corners, which generally means that they should be somewhat brick or block-like. If you can get some cheap quarried stones for corners, buy them. Trying to hunt down good cornerstones is like trying to find "pretty" at a G.O.P. convention; you can spend hours and come up with nothing. During the stone collecting part, cornerstones can be time consuming, and if you feel like you're spending more time on finding them than you would probably like, you most likely are.

Finally, if the stones passed the type, size and shape tests we then took appearance into account. Having an ample supply of stone to choose from, we considered making each wall a certain kind of stone based on type or color, but this meant more time spent fishing through them and grouping. What we settled upon was using the most distinctive stones near doorways and windows, in plain view of everyone using the doors or looking at the windows. It's been four years since we moved into our home and I still notice the coolest looking stones whenever I walk in the door.

Before placing any stone in the forms they need to be washed of any mud, clay, or other stuck-on substances. We had previously hosed them down in the trailer and moved them onto forms. We then washed them off with a short, 3' diameter, metal wash tub. The tub, I think, was purchased at a pet store and is normally used for dog-washing. We kept the bucket filled with water (changing it every 20 or so stones) and scrubbed each quickly with a durable floor scrubbing brush and placed them back on clean, unused forms. If left on the ground, a good rain will send mud splotches all over them. Is this cleaning activity best fit for the obsessive, anal builder, or is it footed in some reality? Most masons will tell you that cleaner stones or bricks form better bonds with concrete. I've been to some brick building construction sites and depending on the quality of the bricks (new or used) some masons can be seen scrubbing the debris off of the bricks that need it. Newly purchased bricks usually don't need cleaning but tend to be expensive to build with.

With our heaping piles of stones cleaned and ready, it was time to start building stone walls. The forms were bolted together, the sand and gravel (¾" gravel stones or less) were close by, and we had two pallets of Portland cement type I, between the sand and gravel heaps. The cement was covered by a waterproof tarp and was set on pallets to keep them dry. Do not let your bags of cement get wet or they'll end up more useless than a priest at a bris.

Here's Annette happily unloading the last batch, wheelbarrow
ramp on right and one corner of the house to the left

We never had any thoughts about mixing the cement in a
wheelbarrow or any other "non-mechanized cement mixing
device." Buy a mixer; it is worth every single worthless penny
you invest in it. We found a great mixer at an equipment rental
store. Call around to see if they have any used models they're
unloading for cheap. Some hardware stores now carry heavy-
plastic mixers that will probably do the job. We used a metal
fabricated mixer and were very happy with it. After each use,
scrape the cement out and keep it clean. There are fins inside
that can gather cement and the build up can prevent the cement
from being mixed thoroughly. We scraped and sprayed the
mixer every night before quitting.

If you haven't installed a well, or you don't yet have
access to clean, debris-free water, then now is the time. A
hose with a hand spigot on the end is crucial for mixing

and cleaning equipment. Our well was drilled one week before we started mixing, and the water quality wasn't good enough at first. We adhered to the international building codes for water mixed with cement. Code stated that water should not contain oils, bases, acids, excess salts, or organic matter. We had to bleed the well and water line of silt that was present after the 220' well was dug. This process took an entire day. We couldn't even spray ourselves down with the chilly water because the silt leaves a thick film on your skin and can turn hair into straw. We had to wait until the water was clear and potable. Most cement mixing companies will tell you to use drinking-quality water for best results.

Before mixing any cement, we sorted through our stones and placed them in the forms to get the best fit between them. After that, we set them up on the forms until they would eventually be cemented in. We did this before we built every section of wall since it allowed us to work faster and we didn't want to be building too many small sections of wall. We would pre-fit the whole section of wall (120' perimeter) with stones that fit snugly together, took them back out and kept them in order. After doing this it was just a matter of mixing cement and, when slightly motivated, I found that building a 25' section of wall 19" high in one day was entirely possible.

We had a fast method for mixing that involved (3) five-gallon buckets, two shovels, and a wheelbarrow. We used, as mentioned earlier, a (1:3:4) mix of cement, sand, and gravel. I spray painted C, S, or G, on the buckets for cement, sand, and gravel, and then filled them with a tripled amount of ingredients. When they had the right amount of shovelfuls of each we then drove a nail through the bucket to mark the correct volume. Instead of having to count out every shovel we simply needed to fill the buckets to the fill-lines. After filling the buckets up to the proper level we dumped them into the mixer without water and let it mix until there was cement throughout the entire batch. Dry ingredients need to be mixed thoroughly before adding water. Doing this ensures the cement will adhere better to the sand and gravel.

We used a fairly dry to slightly moist mix. We could tell how the mix was by grabbing a clump with a gloved hand and squeezing. If it just about stuck together, not crumbly and falling apart or too wet and running out of your hand, then this was a good mixture. You'll notice a need to adjust your water amounts depending on the moisture content of the sand and gravel. After a rainy night our water usage decreased considerably.

According to the height of the house (from the backfill to the sill plate) which was just around 10', we planned on having to move our forms up the wall seven times. The first two vertical sections of wall needed plenty of stones and cement because the basement windows were the only framed structures to take up any other space. We used large stones for the bottom layers and medium to small for the rest of the walls. Having door and window frames in higher sections decreases the amount of stones and cement to be mixed. However, depending on your climate, more windows means less stone wall protecting you from the sub-zero temperatures and Canadian winds. The higher the walls became, the more creative we had to be when it came to moving wheelbarrows of cement mix to an accessible height for shoveling.

Extra forms being used for wheelbarrow ramps,
the spools are wide enough for the ramps and tools

Forms not being used became ramps and scaffolding to hold our stones and heavy loads of cement. We used discarded cable spools as platforms and a series of ramps that enabled us to move loads up to about 8' high.

Part of the wall with doorway opening and impatient dogs

Cement mix drying in the forms, the rock face is to the right with mix
around and behind it. Vertical rebar is in and the cement surface is left rough
for the next pour.

When we filled the forms, we were careful to pack
cement all around the facing stones, with the stones no less
than 2" apart. I advocated using more cement whenever
possible, while Annette stressed the cheaper price of stones,
what with them being free and all. To compromise, we used
larger stones with plenty of concrete between them, behind
and beneath. We were also working around vertical rebar and
horizontal rebar, making sure the cement covered these
completely. When we reached the top of a set of forms we
were filling, the surface of the cement was scuffed-up using a
small trowel. Scuffing the surface as opposed to smoothing
it out, will give the next layer a better grip. Also, at the
junction of two courses, it is important to form a ridge or

slope the surface toward the exterior of the wall, to prevent water from seeping in at this juncture. This is arguably more important with your basement walls but should be considered throughout. If we ever left a course unfinished for more than a day, we poured a pasty mix of cement and water over the last dried section before continuing the course. This helps the two sections adhere better.

After two courses of 16" wide forms we reached the height for our basement ceiling. The 2x4 sill plate, coated with a safe waterproofing substance, needed to be bolted down to the inside top of this layer of wall. To do this, just before the cement started to set, we sunk 12" carriage bolts into the cement every 4'. We made sure that the bolts rose at least 4" vertically from the surface of the cement. The bolts were also placed 1-½" from the inside edge. This would allow us to drill holes in the 2x4's and set them onto the carriage bolts, all along the north and south walls of the house. Only 2-opposing walls need bolts and sill plates. On top of the sill plate is where we'll rest our 2x10 floor joists.

The next set of forms would only be 12" wide to allow for the 4" sill plate. We bolted the outside forms together but needed to move the inside forms inward 4". So, this course was bolted on the outside to the exterior forms, but only braced on the inside. We cut new 12" wooden spacers to set the forms correctly, then wired and braced them as usual. After filling 16" wide forms, the 12" forms were much faster to fill and allowed us to get more of the exterior walls built within the same amount of work hours.

Transition From 16" Wall to 12" Wall

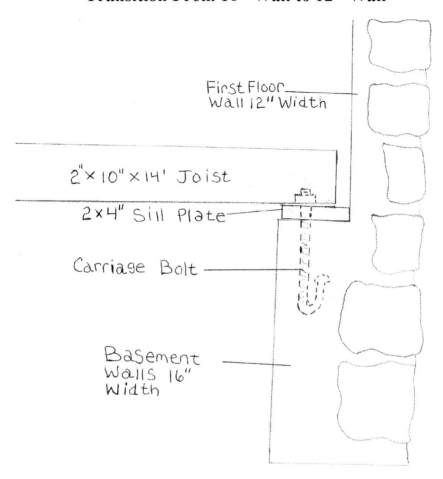

First Floor
Wall 12" Width

2"×10"×14' Joist

2×4" Sill Plate

Carriage Bolt

Basement
Walls 16"
Width

What we needed to do now was prepare some 2x3s for furring strips. These are placed horizontally against the inside set of forms with the wide side against the forms. Like the window and door frames, the furring should have nails on each side except for the one facing the inside forms. We wanted these boards to provide a wood face imbedded in the concrete walls. The exposed wood surface is what we needed to form the base of a nailing surface for our interior walls.

2 x 3 furring strips coated with non-toxic water sealer and cemented
inside the wall. We will nail our interior walls to them.

We were now reaching the level of our window frames.
We set these in the same manner as other frames. The frames
ran vertically up to 3" from the sill plate. We built all around
the frames and finally reached the top of our walls. We
cemented over the frames and made sure to make this top
surface absolutely smooth and level. The sill plate will need
to sit on a completely smooth surface. We imbedded 12"
carriage bolts into the concrete every 4'. The carriage bolts
were bent on a vice, like the j-pins with rebar, to resemble a
big "J" and set 2" from the outside edge of the sill. We
couldn't set carriage bolts where the door and window
frames were so we set them 3" on either side.

The last section of stone wall, the cement is smoothed
over on top for a flat, level surface

Stone walls nearly finished and we started to remove the last two sections
of forms. The small square opening at the top was added to vent warm air
into the house from the greenhouse.

Over the concrete sill we placed a pink, foam sill sealer. This is an insulating material that comes in rolls, and it was rolled over the sill and the carriage bolts were poked right through it. We then cut unplaned 2x10's for the top sill plate. Again, these should be waterproofed and drilled to meet up with the carriage bolts. It is a smart idea to countersink the bolts into the sill so that there are no protrusions which may interfere with your joist and rafter placement. The sill plates were placed on the sill with the bolts sticking up through them. We then placed 2-large washers around the bolts, then nuts, and tightened them down making the sill plate snug with the surface of the concrete. We made sure to align the 2x10's with the outside edge of the stone walls since the rafters will be sitting on them.

Stone walls are finished, the sill plate is on and we have the built up beam resting on the sill, over the door frame.

Here is the south face of the house; the greenhouse will be built in front.

Our stone walls were now finished. Annette didn't have the back problems that I had, so finishing the walls was met with much celebration on my part. It was a beautifully clear and cool night toward the end of November, and all seemed right; except for the sad fact that a coke-snortin' evangelical and his inbred brother in Florida had just stolen the White House and the country from under our noses while we worked.

Chapter Six

Setting the Columns, Girders, Floor Joists, and Subfloor

It was after the fourth section of stone wall was finished that we decided to build the first floor of the house. In the previous chapter I discussed building the stone walls up to the sill plate for continuity. Mixing the material in this chapter in between the stone work, Annette and I decided, would be somewhat confusing. For the sake of clarity we separated the material.

When we reached the first sill plate and the 12" section of wall we were able to install the first floor. To do this we needed columns, girders, 2x10 floor joists, and ¾" plywood (v-notch) for the sub floor. We began by setting the columns in a small mound of cement at the base. They were placed over the spray painted marks indicating the center of the pier footings. This kept the columns vertical while we installed the girders. We used three columns and needed to line them up accurately down the center of the basement. We put a nail in the sill plate, in the exact midpoint of the wall, on both opposing walls. We then tied a piece of string to both nails and made sure the string was tight and straight across the basement; this was our guide for the columns and we placed them directly underneath the string in a straight line.

The columns come with 4"x4" metal plates that, for some reason, are not welded onto the ends. These plates were placed on the top of each column to act as a platform for the 8x10 girders that we used. There are holes in each corner of the plates and we screwed lag bolts through these into the undersides of the girders. When setting the columns, we used a 6' carpenter's level to make them plumb and then propped 2x4's against them to hold them still until the mix at the base dried. Once this was dry we were ready to lay the girders on top.

With a rented engine hoist, Annette could properly set girders by herself, two large eyehooks are screwed into either end and the chain connected to them.

Moving the heavy girders was a snap with the hoist.

We bought 8x10 girders at a local sawmill simply because they were the best price at the time. We could have used 6x10's to cover the 8' distances between the columns, but at a better price we again decided to overbuild. Having only two people to set girders, instead of a small crew, I decided to rent an engine hoist. We propped it on top of some unused forms to reach the height needed to lift the girders over the columns. The nice thing about the hoist is the maneuverability. We lowered the heavy girders using a large link chain hooked up to eyehooks screwed into the tops of the girders. We could then raise or lower the girders to exactly where we needed them. Annette was able to set a heavy 8x10 girder by herself safely using the engine hoist.

With a nudge here and there we were ready to align the girders
and connect them with metal fasteners

One end of the girder sets on the sill plate, not on a 2x4
sill plate but right on the cement. We waterproofed the girder
end first and a piece of aluminum flashing was placed
between the girder and cement to keep any moisture away
from the wood. Code actually states that the ends of wood
girders touching concrete walls should have ½" air space
around the top, both sides and the end unless the end is
waterproofed. It also says that adjoining ends should be
cross-tied to each other, or inter-tied by caps or ties. This is
from the international building codes manual and should be
adhered to. The other end of the girder rested on one of those
precariously placed 4"x4" metal plates that, for some brain-
dead reason still aren't attached to the ends of the lolly
columns. The two middle girders were placed end- to-end
and according to code were fastened together with thick,

metal strapping. Our middle column was slightly higher due to the pad not being smoothed over enough in that spot. Yeah, I took hell for it and notched the bottom of one girder with a chainsaw to allow for the column's extra height. We fastened all the girders together and were ready to hang the floor joists.

Again, the floor joists we used were 2x10's (see chart). The actual distance from the sill plate to the side of the girder was 12'6", so we bought (57) 2x10x14's and cut them down to size. This job can be done in an assembly line fashion with two people. One can measure and mark the boards, while the other can cut and stack them in the basement. The job of measuring, cutting, and stacking over 50 boards can become a bit tedious. Remember the old adage, "measure twice and cut once?" Or how about that other one, "lift with your nose and not your appendix," or something like that. Anyway, try to remember them both; they may be of very little use to you some night at a cocktail party.

With the boards all cut, we stretched the tape measure lengthwise along the connected girders, end to end, and marked every 16", for the placement of the joists. We then did the same to the sill plate by marking the front of the 2x4 with a Sharpie. This makes it easy and accurate when lining up the joists

Purchase some joist hangers for 2x10's and enough 8d, 10d and 12d nails to get them up. I propped one end of the joist on the sill plate and the other on top of a 4' high cable spool. I also used a spool on the other end, under the sill plate, and then ran ladder from one spool to the other. This made a convenient bridge which saved time jumping down from one spool and climbing the other. At the girder end, I wrapped the joist hanger around the bottom of the joists and nailed them down to the girder with the 8d nails in the appropriate holes and 10d, 12d, 16d or whatever the hangers call for in their appropriate holes. The joists are toe-nailed down to the sill plate using (3) 8d nails. Code states that only (3) 8d nails are required to fasten a joist to a girder, but if you go with the joist hangers, you can actually get 8-nails into the girder with the pre-set holes in the hangers. The floor will creak less with more nail support.

The floor joists are in and we're covering them with plywood.

We had a basement opening planned for a stairway and needed to double up the 2x10s by pounding two together with 10d nails, one every foot on both sides of the joist. All sides of the opening have double joists (trimmers and headers), this is code also. If an opening is going to be longer than 11', then column supports should be used under the trimmers. If an opening is smaller for a chimney, we still need to double our trimmers and headers (the short boards connecting the trimmers). When hanging many joists, alternately nail them on both sides of the girder to decrease any movement of the girders when nailing into them. When all the joists were toe-nailed to the sill plate and fastened with hangers at the girders, we decided to cut up some leftover 2x10 pieces for "blocking".

Some carpenters will tell you that blocking is unnecessary if the joists are hung properly, but some codes still require it. When blocking, we're wedging scraps of 2x10 pieces cut to fit between the joists. The blocking pieces should be placed in the center of the joists where they provide more resistance to joist twisting. The way we did it was to snap a chalk line down the center of the joists (on the bottom edges) and alternated the blocking on either side of the chalk line. The blocking scraps were nailed down with 10d nails and some finger parts. The work space between joists is not very accommodating and sometimes fingertips are mistaken for nails. At this point we were anxious to get the sub floor in; with the first floor finished we could move the rest of the exterior wall building inside, instead of working on platforms around the perimeter.

For a sub floor we used ¾", v-notch plywood. I don't recommend using pressboard for anything, maybe a coffin, but not for house construction. Pressboard is absolute garbage and I wouldn't build a chicken coop with it--having more respect for the animals' welfare.

The first floor subfloor is in, and we are ready to build up from here.

The ¾" plywood that we bought came in 4'x8' sheets and had notched ends that help when aligning them. They are nailed down with 8d flooring nails, one every 6" on the outer ends and every 10" inside the board. International code calls for every 12", but nails are cheap and we wanted a tight, creak-free floor. And, with a hardass supervisor like "Surly" the cattle hound watching over our progress, we were constantly ignoring codes and overbuilding whenever possible. If a flooring nail seemed an inch or so over spaced, we'd get nipped in the lower thigh or calf area; his way of always trying to keep us in line. Damned clever dog. Someday our species will be smarter than theirs...someday.

If you've never nailed down a plywood sub floor, there are two protective devices that you will need: a set of knee pads and safety goggles. Simply place a knee pad over each eye and wrap the goggles smugly around the knees while you...oops, what an idiot. I misspelled snugly. These safety devices are self-explanatory. And, if you calculate the cheap price of both as opposed to emergency room surgery for a chipped knee bone or nail-pierced retina (particularly during the reign of George II, a man who'd rather bomb people with our money than offer affordable health care), the pads and goggles are worth it.

The plywood will need some sawing to fit it properly. We used the circular saw with a good plywood cutting blade and a chalk line to mark the boards. For example, if a board needed to be cut at 4', we'd measure 4' from one end of the board then do the same on the other side. We'd then snap a chalk line between the two points. The boards were placed on two spools and then we cut along the chalk line. Try to be as accurate as possible when cutting, this eliminates the dreaded second-cutting. This can be tricky when dealing with 1/8" and having to shear that amount off of a 4' piece of plywood.

We nailed our boards down so that the joints were staggered. This is customary and meets code standards. Two boards next to each other wouldn't end on the same joist, and according to code, the boards should span no less than 3 joists. So, when coming close to an edge, prepare to cut the more interior board shorter leaving three joists to be spanned. In other words, don't cut a 16" wide piece of plywood planning to nail the edges down between two joists only. This decreases the strength of the plywood flooring.

When we finished the flooring, we decided to spend the night in comfy sleeping bags on the new floor. Normally we'd be cramped in the small camper with our dogs and whatever cat wanted to stay in for the night. With the floor finished we thought that we'd enjoy it while it was clean and new-looking, because the next day it would be covered with cement debris, gravel, dust, and plenty of tools as we began the exterior stone walls.

CHAPTER SEVEN

CEILING JOISTS, BUILT UP BEAMS, FIRST FLOOR COLUMNS

I f you've decided after building your stone walls that you'd like only one floor for living space, then now would be the time to start building your roof. If this is what some of you may be doing, then skip to Chapter Nine if you'd like; that's where we explain how we framed the roof.

When our exterior walls were finished we were ready to frame the second floor. This is done much like the first floor. We used 2x10s again for joists, but this time we used a built up beam to connect them to as well as wood posts (6x6's) for columns to support the beam. We used (3) 6x6 columns, one placed in the center, and one on each side, halfway between the sill plate and center column. We cut 6x6 square holes in the sub floor just above the basement girders so we could set the wooden columns right on the girders. Then the columns were toe nailed down to the girders to keep them somewhat stable while placing the built up beam on top.

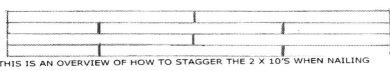

THIS IS AN OVERVIEW OF HOW TO STAGGER THE 2 X 10'S WHEN NAILING THEM TOGETHER FOR A BUILT UP BEAM.

We placed our built-up beam on the sill plates and three 6x6 posts.
I cut holes in the plywood and sat the posts directly on the girders;
notice the three horizontal rows of furring in the walls.

With the built up beam in place, we set the joists 16" apart and used
hangers to fasten them; we nailed a 2x4 ledger to the posts just
beneath the joists. We could rest one end on the ledger while
the other end was being toenailed to the sill plate.

When building a built-up beam, it is important to pay attention to the spacing of the joints, or junctions between boards. There should be at least 16" between joints on adjacent boards. Also, you must pay careful attention to your nailing pattern. There should be (3) 16 or 20 D nails on the edge of each board, and 16 or 20 d nails should be spaced diagonally across from each other every 10" or so.

The span between the sill plate and center of the top of the 6x6 post was 13'10", so we used 2x10x14's and cut them to fit. We nailed 3 of these together using 16d nails. We then set one end on the 2x6 sill plate and the other end on the post. In all, we used (12) 2x10x10'4" boards to connect the posts and sill plates with our built up beam. At the sill plates, we toe nailed the beam down with (6) 16d nails and metal strapping to connect or tie together the ends of the built up 2x10's on the outside of the built up beam. We checked the columns to see if they were plumb and then toe nailed the beam down to the tops of the columns with more 16d nails. The sill plate end of the beam lined up with the outer edge of the sill plate on both sides of the house. With the beam in place we began the tedious process of cutting (57) 2x10x14's for ceiling joists.

Like the first floor joists, the second floor joists are spaced every 16" on center and it helps to mark the front of the sill plate and the top of the built up beam every 16" with a Sharpie. This way the joists can be lined up as close to "on center" as possible. We started with joists lined up flush with the outer edge of the sill plate then toe nailed them down perpendicular to the beam and all along the sill plate every 12". We then used joist hangers to connect one end to the beam and angle ties with (4) 12d nails to fasten the other end to the sill plate. The sill plate end of the joist was measured and cut to be flush with the outer edge of the sill plate and will eventually be fastened to the roof rafters.

We planned for one stairway opening in the blue prints and the much smaller chimney opening. The joists needed to be doubled around these openings with extra trimmers and headers. The chimney openings require 2" between the chimney block and wood; we have 16"x20" chimney blocks and our openings allow for 2" all around the blocks.

The stairway opening was planned to be a standard width of 3'2" wide. Annette also designed the opening to run parallel to the joists (on both floors); stairway openings require more planning and trickier carpentry when they run perpendicular to the joists. The length of the opening was based on the "run" of the stairway. An explanation of stairway building is found in Chapter Eight. The run was actually 9' and we wanted to allow at least 7' for headroom above the bottom stair.

Framing an Opening in the Floor

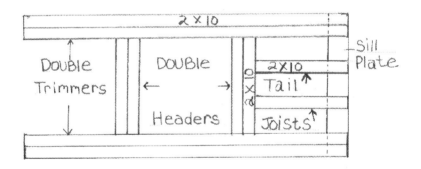

Since our stairway opening was 3'2", we first set our inside trimmers this distance apart. The next cut was the 3'2" header, and we made two of these. The first header was placed between the inside trimmers and nailed down with 10d nails. This was the inside header and we placed it at the distance measured for the length of the opening, which was 9'. We then nailed the second header behind the first; not the side of the stairway opening. The two outside trimmers came next, and were nailed to the inside trimmers. The space between the inside trimmers and behind the headers required two tail joists which were nailed at one end to the 3'2" outside header and the other end to the rim.

When hanging the joists, plan to leave space in your designs for installing the opening before the other joists are in place. This will give you much needed working room. The extra room comes in handy when trying to pound 16d nails into headers and trimmers with no joists in the way minimizing the swinging range of the hammer.

There is another consideration when hanging the joists. If you've designed any walls upstairs or downstairs that run parallel to the joists below them and are load-bearing partitions, then reinforcement between the joists will be necessary. There are 2 acceptable means of doing this, one being more work intensive yet necessary when the load-bearing wall falls directly between 2 joists (Hint: try not to design your load-bearing walls this way). You will need to cut more blocking from scraps of 2x10 floor joists and place these 16" on-center between the two joists that will bear the load. If the load-bearing wall is designed to fall directly over a floor joist, then this is reinforced by simply doubling the joist or even tripling it. Tripling the joists will ensure solid flooring for heavy loads. If you buy the good plywood for a sub floor such as 3/4" or 5/8", then you won't need reinforcement for non-load-bearing walls.

The latest figures for weights of bathroom fixtures that I've received ranged from 10 PSF (pounds per square foot) for vanities and toilets, to 20 PSF for tubs and another 30 PSF for a tile floor with mortar for its setting. Under the smaller fixtures you can cut blocking and double this up on both sides underneath them. Basically, we made 4 blockers and placed two between the joists under one side of the tub or vanity and two underneath the opposing side. When reinforcing the tub, we doubled up our joists underneath the tub edges because it ran parallel to them. If you need to drill into any joists for plumbing or electrical requirements, then drill in the middle of the joist since this is where the bending forces acting upon a joist are minimal. If there are designs for a tiled floor, then double up each joist and place two sub floors beneath. One ½" plywood sub floor with a 5/8" plywood sub floor on top will prevent the floor from moving and possibly cracking the mortar around the tiles.

If you have planned for a large wood stove like we did, in the middle of the first floor, then this should be reinforced too. We had an early 1900's cast iron cook stove planned for the house, so we reinforced the 3 joists underneath by doubling them. We've since switched over to an outdoor wood furnace and hot water, radiant floor heating. So, the joists are overbuilt for the stove that no longer provides us with old fashioned cooking, some smoke, and plenty of dust in the living room. Good riddance to old fire hazards.

When the joists were set and the openings properly reinforced, the task of moving 30 sheets of 3/4" plywood to the second floor loomed over us. With two people this can be a physically draining activity, so finding the easiest route for the plywood is the best thing to plan for. When they were brought up to the second floor we placed them roughly where they would be nailed down. This gave us some better footing when working on top of the joists, and we could walk without fear of falling painfully between them.

After the plywood was arranged on the joists we lifted one sheet at a time and glued the tops of joists with wood adhesive. This helps prevent creaky sub floors and we applied it to the joists underneath the first floor sub floor as well. We aligned the tongue and grooves and nailed them down with 8d flooring nails. Like the first floor sub floor we left 1/8" gaps between the tongue and groove edges and 1/16" gaps between the 4' ends. These gaps are factory recommended to allow for expansion when heated. A plywood distributor near us recommended a 1/4" bead of glue along the grooved edge but we didn't hear of this recommendation until the sub floor was finished and truthfully, our edges don't creak after 4 plus year of walking on them.

Annette cutting a piece of ¾ inch plywood. Notice the safety goggles and Knee pads she painstakingly ignored. The joist just beneath the board she's cutting has been doubled for the stairway opening, with a doubled header board running perpendicular to the doubled joists.

I cut the boards and Chris nailed them down. Notice his invisible, super hero safety goggles and knee pads; you need to be a certified super hero to own these.

After installing the floorboards we decided to build our stairway, giving us easier access than the ladders we'd been using to reach the second floor. We also covered a majority of the first floor stairway opening to the basement with extra pieces of plywood to avoid any spine crushing, unexpected falls. The large cable spools we used for platforms were moved up to the second floor for the roof project and we reasoned that we needed a stairway as soon as possible; the ladders had become unsafe for carrying heavy materials.

CHAPTER EIGHT

STAIRWAY

The word "stairway" has, through the linguistic ages, come to represent many different concepts to many different people. Jimmy Page wrote a song about one. Some religious folks believe in a golden one, and most Americans would rather be probed by Hitler's dead, rotting tongue than use one when an elevator is available. But I did my own research and found this bit of information about the word "stairway." It is in fact a compound word, having both Greek and Latin origins. The Oxford English Dictionary describes the first part of the word as having been used, in fact, in Ancient Greece and the earliest translation they've been able to come up with is the word, "pain." The second part of the word, "way", from the Latin, is most commonly translated by most modern linguists as the phrase, "in the ass." Unfortunately, I discovered this information after we built the stairway, but I can still say that without performing your own highly flawed etymology of the word as I've done, the Ancients in their transcendent wisdom were really on to something.

Building a stairway correctly can unnerve an astronaut on morphine. It is not for the worker who likes to accomplish plenty of work in a normal day. Okay, I know the people who build stairways have wisely tuned me out already. These people build them for a living and could design one in a drunken slumber simply by sticking a pencil in their hands when they're passed out. To the majority of people out there, building a stairway is something they will never have to do. Although cool looking and giving insight to the creator, a stairway should most often be left to the good carpenters who won't foolishly hack into an expensive 2x12 knowing that it will surely become screwed up. Seriously, don't fudge around with this if you're in a rush to move into your home like we were. I can offer the basics for information, but the detail work should be finished when the roof is on and there is time to curse every religious icon since the beginnings of recorded history.

Annette, through the miracle of reading, and watching a stairway building video that I rented, took the time to learn the specifics of stair building while I finished the upstairs flooring. So when I'm through babbling she can run you through it. Some parts of our stairway weren't meant to be permanent. The 3 carriages (the 2x12's cut into stairs) were staying but the treads weren't. We used 2x10's for the treads cut into 3'2"lengths (the width of the stairway opening) and nailed them down with 12d nails onto the carriages. Beautiful maple or oak boards can be used later to detail the treads and the risers as well. We didn't want to put finished treads down and ruin them with the work traffic and all the construction debris we'd be throwing down on them.

For a professionally detailed stairway, I suggest that you do what we did and rent a video on finishing stairways. The carpenters in some of these videos are masters and spend more time on detailing stairways then on the most rudimentary of bodily functions.

Stairway Details

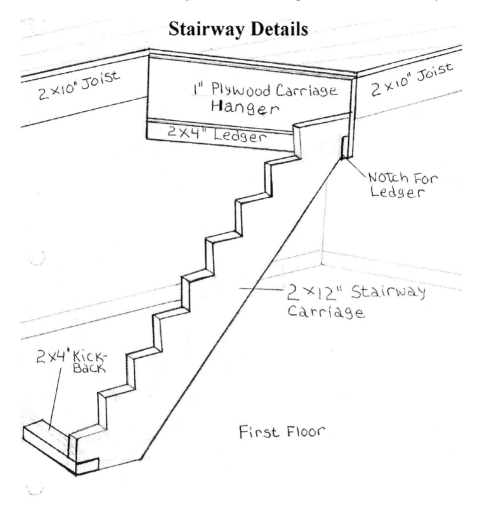

To save room, spiral stairways can be an option, or adding a platform midway with a right, left, or U-turn can help. After we built our stairway straight (for simplicity's sake and to enable moving material up them more easily), we decided some time later that we wanted more living room in the, uh, living room.

We decided to add a platform midway up the stairs and turn it toward the kitchen and away from the living room. This also gave us more room in the upstairs living room since we could install joists between the previous opening and add flooring over that. Downstairs we added 17" more of walking room which doesn't sound like much but it really does make a difference. If you can imagine the width of Rush Limbaugh's mouth in its normal, relaxed state then this will give you a fair estimate of how much room we've added by doing this to our stairway.

We also removed that early 1900's cast iron cooking stove (mostly because it was in the way of the new stairway bend) that was in the middle of the first floor. As far as those old stoves go, I'd have to say that I'd strongly recommend one if you want to burn your whole house down. Seriously, though, you might as well pour gasoline on your floor and spark it, or just go out and insult a Sicilian.

One ingenious stairway we have seen is a spiral stairway built of self-hewn logs. The logs were arranged into an ascending spiral with a pole running vertically through one end of each log to fasten them. It was inexpensive, very appealing, and an efficient use of space.

Well, that's my shtick on stairways. Being a clever reader I'm sure that you are fully aware by now that I know very little about building them. While I may stand in awe of the perfect stairway and have fallen down a few after open bar events and Phish concerts, I still harbor a certain distaste for them as well. Oh, and for some other things, too. Yeah, like Limbaugh's mouth. I know it has nothing to do with building a stairway…actually I'm pretty sure it does. All of it does, particularly the part about the one-eyed prostitute and that man of the Polish persuasion. Anyhow, Annette knows what the hell she's talking about, having shown me how to build our stairway.

This is actually easier than mutton head tries to let on (Annette here). To build a rough, utility stairway, start with your stairwell (opening between floors) framed in with doubled joists on either side, and your header boards doubled as well. You will need 3 long (14' or more) 2x12 boards (get more than three if you're sure you're going to hack at least one). Measure the distance between the surfaces of the floors (first floor to second floor) to be bridged with your stairway. Remember to take into account your finished floor if this is not already installed, by adding 3/4" to your total (assuming you will be installing wood, tile, or other flooring of considerable thickness). Take your measurement and divide this number by your desired rise or height of step. This is the number of stairs you will have. To determine your desired rise, first understand that most rises are between 8" and 9". Also, the combination of rise (vertical rise of each step) and run (depth or length of step) is typically no more than 17". Another factor to consider is that the lower your rise the longer your overall carriage length will need to be in order to bridge the same distance.

First, I'll describe how we found the rise for our stairway. As an example, our height from sub floor to sub floor between the first and second floors was 99-3/4". Since our floors were not finished, to this we added 3/4" to adjust for the eventual finished floor to obtain 100-1/2" for a total rise (distance from top of first floor to top of second floor). We selected a rise of 8-1/4" for each step, and divided this into our total height of 100-1/2", for a total of 12.18". We then took our figure of 12.18" and rounded down to 12, meaning we needed 12 steps total. Now, with a total rise of 100-1/2 inches, we divided this by our 12 steps and ended up with a rise of 8.375" (or 8 -3/8"); slightly more than we desired but still a comfortable height to work with, remembering that the length of the average riser is between 8" and 9".

Next, determine your run, or length of step. The run is a measure of the length or depth of the treads, or the boards we will be walking on. We subtracted the amount for our rise (8 3/8") from 17 to obtain 8 5/8", the measure of our treads; remember that you could choose a higher or lower rise as you desire. I'm not sure who decided 17 was the magic number for the sum of the rise and run or what their motive was, and it's your house, so do as you please while remembering that a longer run will cause your stairway to take up more living space.

It is helpful to sketch your stairway and check your math at this point. Also, using your sketch, check to make sure, that at no point does the distance between any stair tread and your framed stairwell equal less than 6'8". This figure is an important one; it makes sure that people coming down your stairway don't bump their heads.

Once you have your figures for your rise and run, you are ready to start marking your carriages for cutting. This is done carefully with a carpenter's square, to mark the area to be cut, and either a board attached to the square with clamps or handy little devices called stair buttons (or stair gauges), which are less bulky and so are easier to work with.

Measuring the Cuts for the Carriage

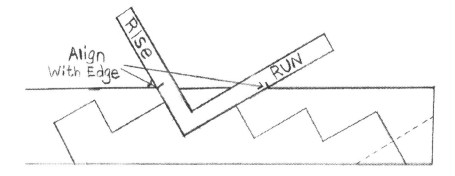

Draw out your desired number of stairs on your 2x12, take a deep breath, and get cutting. We found this job was most simply done with a circular saw to make the longer cuts, and a jigsaw to notch out the corners that the circular saw couldn't complete without cutting too far into your boards. When you are finished cutting your stairs (double and triple check that your calculations are correct now), cut off the extra and square off your ends with a carpenter's square. Doing this creates the end cuts that will meet up with your carriage hanger board on the high end and sub floor on the other. Before you do this, remember to take 1" off the length of your top stair (run) to compensate for the thickness of your hanger board. After doing this give the stair carriage a test run to see if it fits. You may also want to add a bit to the rise (height) of your bottom step by using temporary shims to compensate for your eventual finished floor's height. Another important step is to reduce the overall height of your lowermost riser to compensate for the thickness of your tread.

The final step in cutting your carriages is to notch out at both the top and bottom an 1 1/2" x 3 1/2" area where the kick plate and ledger will meet up with the carriages (see drawing). A helpful if rather obvious hint here; cut one of your carriages in the manner described, test it for fit, and then use this first one as a template for the rest.

Once we finished copying the other two, we attached our carriages with 16d's and nailed down the temporary treads which Chris described earlier. This is how we built our stairs and it's pretty much the standard method, but not necessarily how you might want to build yours. Some research on your own here could uncover simpler methods and materials. Did I happen to note, by the way, that there are factory prefabricated stairways that you can purchase? If you're still intimidated by the thought of doing this by yourself, some hardware stores may be able to supply you with pre-fab stairway carriages. This could actually save you the trouble and possibly the expense of destroying a 2x12.

CHAPTER NINE

SETTING UP RIDGE BOARD, HOW TO CUT RAFTERS AND INSTALL THEM

When we finished the second floor sub floor, the days were pretty short and our work time limited. Compared to large-stone masonry, the carpentry part of the house was about as easy as rigging the Florida elections. The original plans called for stone walls formed into gable ends reminiscent of an old English or Scottish style. It was mid to late November, the water was nasty cold to work with, and we found our hands were getting bloodied easier. Making the gable ends out of wood was much, much more expensive, but the weather set the agenda for us.

The roof, gable ends, and dormer were framed up in just over a week. Building a house with wood is infinitely faster than stone masonry and seeing the upstairs put together so quickly gave us the mental and physical boost we needed.

Roof trusses were never really an option, since neither of us could understand why someone would pay so much for constructed trusses and then lose attic space completely. Roof rafters are not excessively heavy to work with like trusses, and they can be set by two people. Working at a good pace, a two-person crew can completely rafter a house in less than 3 days. Ours took more time due to the shed dormer and our work schedules. We both needed to schedule time off to work on the rafters, and use all the daylight we could.

We began by fastening our ridge board to 2x4 vertical studs. The studs were used to support the ridge board and keep it plumb until the rafters were in. These studs were nailed to the sill plate.

We used a 2 x 4 x 12 for the vertical support and a diagonal 2 x 3 to keep the ridge from moving side to side. This support can be either temporarily nailed or screwed into the sill plate. Before securing the end to the sill plate, we needed to place a level against the vertical 2 x 4 to make sure this was plumb.

Setting Ridge Board Over Sill Plate

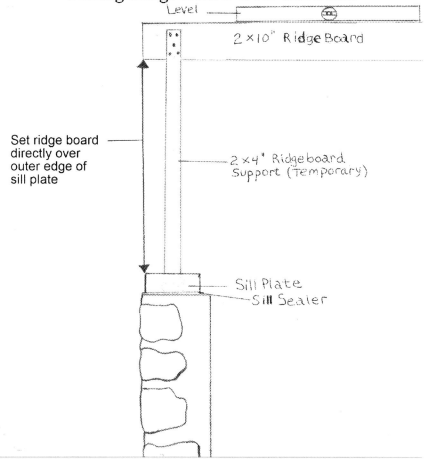

Level

2 × 10" Ridge Board

Set ridge board directly over outer edge of sill plate

2 × 4" Ridgeboard Support (Temporary)

Sill Plate
Sill Sealer

The ridge board was made with (2) 2x10x20s to cover the 32' width of the house, east to west. We cut this down to exactly 32' and cut the east end flush with the sill plate. We used a plumb bob to line this up. I had helped a friend frame up a roof for a small cabin years ago and he taught me a quick and precise way to find the angle cuts on the rafters without suffering through the Pythagorean formulas. We then took a scrap of 2x10 and cut off (2) 2' pieces for connecting or coupling the ridge board at the center. The pieces we nailed on each side of the ridge board with 16d nails and to stop the board from flapping in the wind, we erected a 6X6 vertical wood post underneath the coupling. We used 90° metal braces to fasten the coupling to the post and the ridge board was much more secure.

The ridgeboard was supported by a 6 x 6 post in
the middle as well as 2 x 4's on the ends.

Our plans called for 7' ceilings upstairs and we wanted accessible attic space to stuff in plenty of insulation. For this, our ridge board needed to be around 11' high. Setting up the ridge board was made easy with the cable spools to stand on. The spools offer plenty of surface area to walk on and store tools, nails or whatever, and they'll never tip over like a ladder set up.

When setting up the ridge board we used an 8' carpenter's level taped to the top to keep it from falling off. The ridge board needs to be perfectly level from one end to the other. When trying to get it level we raised or lowered it while holding it up against the vertical 2x4 support. When it reached the level point, we marked the 2x4 where it met the bottom of the ridge board and screwed it down with a drill and 3" wood screws. Trying to pound a 2x4 into a ridge board can become difficult and can also throw off the accuracy. A variable speed drill with a Phillips head bit makes this activity much smoother. Simply hold the ridge board against the 2x4 and zip the wood screws in.

We also cut some scrap 2x4's for bracing the vertical 2x4 supports. We adjusted the supports until the ridge board was perfectly level, we then screwed the smaller 2x4 braces into them and the sill plate. This kept the ridge board from moving laterally.

After the ridge board was secure we needed to frame up the 7' high x 20' long shed dormer. We did on the south side and used 2x4x8's for our wall studs and top sill plate. The wall framing part was easy and like the joists we spaced the studs 16" on-center and cut them to a height of 6'9", allowing 3" for the sill plate 2x4 and the lower one. Annette had designed the dormer with (2) 3'x4' windows and the picture shows them framed up on either side of it.

She found the windows in a company catalogue so we knew just how wide to cut and set the upper and lower studs when framing them in. If your plans are for a simple gable roof and no dormers, your job will be much easier and quicker. With the dormer came shorter roof rafters on top and even shorter jack rafters as well. The jack rafters are nailed into the 2x4 studs used for framing the dormer wall. The jack rafters were installed after the full length rafters and nailed in place at the same angle as them. This allowed for continuity when we covered the rafters afterward with the roofing.

The shed dormer is framed with 2 x 4's spaced 16" apart, on center. We have two window openings and the strapping for the roof is nailed down over the jack rafters.

With the dormer wall in place we could start setting our rafters on both sides of the ridge board. As with the floor joists, we installed a rafter on the north side of the ridge board and one directly on the opposing south side. When installing rafters, always nail down a corresponding rafter on each side of the ridge board to prevent bending or curving. Also, when building with long, expensive boards try to make certain that you're not using cracked, warped, or excessively knotty ones. They should be as straight as possible and have no knots on the outer edges especially. Seriously, a 2x6x 20 is not something you want falling apart on you when you're trying to install it. They're cumbersome and expensive, so try to choose only the best if possible. Fortunately, we purchased our wood supply before the resident-criminal-president forced the Iraq war on us and wood prices soared due to the military buying up all the construction grade wood to "rebuild Halliburton," oops, I mean, "rebuild Iraq."

The north side rafters were all the same length since the dormer was on the south side. I mentioned earlier about cutting the ridge board and aligning the end directly over the outer edge of the sill plate. This was done to get precise pencil marks for the usual rafter cuts. We wanted some overhang, or to leave a tail on the rafters, so we didn't bother cutting them down from their 20' length just yet. The rafters need to be cut at angles flush with the ridge board, the top of the sill plate and with a special cut, the outside edge of the sill plate. The cut at the ridge board end is called the plumb cut. The sill plate end has 2 cuts: one called the plumb at the plate, and the plumb cut at the wall or outer sill plate edge. When these 2 cuts are combined they're known as the bird's mouth.

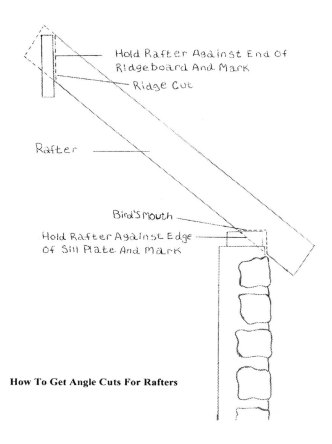

Hold Rafter Against End Of Ridgeboard And Mark

Ridge Cut

Rafter

Bird's Mouth

Hold Rafter Against Edge Of Sill Plate And Mark

How To Get Angle Cuts For Rafters

When we needed the length of the rafters for ordering, we took a tape measure and I held one end at the center of the width of the ridge board and Annette held the other end extending over the ridge plate. This gave us a close approximation of the rafters' length. The length was just over 17', so we knew to order 20' rafters. With the cable spool placed underneath the ridge board at the end, I held the uncut rafter against the end of the ridge board while Annette held the sill plate end. She lined up the rafter against the outer edge of the sill plate with the bottom edge of the rafter meeting the top inner corner of the sill plate and the lower outer edge (see illustration). This will give the rafter a good surface to sit on. With her end of the rafter held in place against the sill plate and my end held tightly in place against the ridge board, we marked the rafters at both ends giving us the exact marks on the rafter. Once we marked the rafter, we cut it and tested it. It fit perfectly and we didn't waste time on the traditional "rise and run" calculations and time wasting math, which may, after cutting, not come out as exact.

If I hadn't learned the quick rafter method from a friend I would have surely wasted one or two perfectly expensive rafters. There are entire chapters written about how to make the angle cuts on rafters involving several measurements, mathematical calculations, and extra money spent on the equipment to do so. Two people can get precise rafter angle cuts in less than five minutes with carpenter's pencils only.

Once we cut our prototype we needed 25 more and copied them from this. To get the length and angles of the rafters covering the shed dormer, we went through the same procedure, only lining up the rafter ends with the ridge plate and the top of the dormer sill plate this time. This length was much shorter and the sill plate angles weren't as acute as the angles for the full length rafters. Again we cut and tested the rafter and made 20 copies.

With the ridgeboard in, we then set all the rafters. They are spaced 16 inches apart, on center. The strapping is on and two roof panes have been installed.

I then marked the ridge board 16" on-center from east to west on both sides, and started nailing the rafters down. The ridge board end was toe nailed using (4) 16d nails. The sill plate end was toe nailed down flush with the outer edge of the plate on all four corners of the house with (4) 12d nails in each. The rest of the rafters were installed one on each side of the ridge board, with the top of the rafter meeting up with the top of the ridge board. This ensures a nice, flat surface for the roof sheathing without making a bulge at the ridge board.

At the sill plate, the rafters were nailed to the floor joists and toe nailed with 12d nails to the sill plate. We then decided to use some of the extra 6" bolts, nuts, and washers from holding the wood forms together, drilled through the rafter and joist, and bolted each one on the north side of the house. We didn't need to do this, but it just made us feel better after doing it.

On the south side where the dormer is, we needed 6 full-length rafters. These had the same angle cuts as the north side, and we attached them to the ridge plate, sill plate, joists, and one on each side of the dormer nailed to the 2x4 stud. With all the full-length rafters and dormer rafters in place we had to cut the jack rafters and set those in, below the dormer rafters.

The smaller jack rafters are nailed into the
vertical 2 x 4 studs used to frame the dormer wall.

The jack rafters were set at the same angle as the full-length rafters and we made the cuts the same as well. First, we measured the distance from the dormer wall studs to the sill plate and allowed an extra 2' for the tail (much of which we cut off the next spring to make room for the solar greenhouse roof).

We used 12d nails to nail the jack rafters to the 2x4 studs and the sill plate. This job went quickly due to the easier handling of the smaller rafters. After maneuvering 17-1/2' rafters, the jack rafters were more like Popsicle sticks.

With rafter spans that are very long there's greater possibility of the roof frame bowing unless rafters are braced. Roof braces, otherwise known as "collar ties," are 2x6s that we nailed from the north side rafters to the south side. These were nailed together with (5) 16ds at each end and placed at a height of 7'1". The collar ties would also act as our ceiling joists and the reason we placed them at 7'1" high, was to allow for a 7' ceiling and the drywall covering. To align the collar ties evenly across the rafters, we used a chalk line held against the rafters at the height of 7'1" and snapped a straight line across. We then lined up the bottom of the 2x6 ties with the blue chalk line on each rafter, and nailed them across making sure that they were level.

Sectional View Of East Side

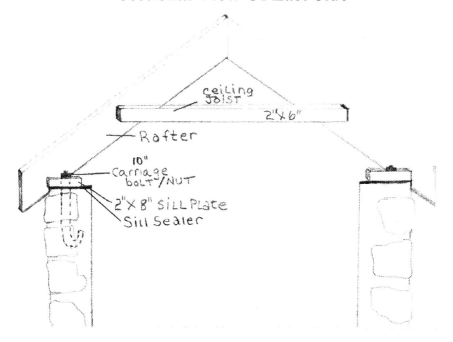

The collar ties, when doing what they're supposed to do, actually take most of the outward push of the roof weight off the exterior walls, prevent the ridge board from sagging, and act as ceiling joists for the second floor. If you don't want your roof to sag like it was framed by inbred, moonshine-guzzling hicks, then collar ties are for you. When nailing them in place we skipped a rafter to allow for the 2'x2' concrete chimney blocks that would be installed after the roof and windows were finished. The collar ties are easily installed and considering the fact that they're doing three important jobs, they are worth every penny.

Annette and I agreed that this chapter was important enough to warrant a quick summary. We used 2x10x20s for a ridge board and scraps of 2x10s to couple them in the middle. This was supported in the center by a 6"x6" post and 2x4s on either end, nailed down to the sill plate. The ridge board was raised to a height of 10'91/4" which allowed for our small attic space and 7' high ceilings. We made certain the ridge board was level then screwed the 2x4 supports to it. The rafter angle was found by holding one end against the end of the ridge board, the other end against the sill plate and pencil marks were made at the intersections of the ridge board and outer sill plate. Rafters are nailed down with one on each side of the ridge board as we go across to prevent bending of the ridge board. Collar ties were attached from the north side rafters to the south side, leaving room for the chimney opening.

I won't fudge with you about rafter installation. It takes some patience and steady hands. Also, if you want to feel safer while working on the roof ridge end, a rock-climber's rope and harness roped off to 2 heavy eye hooks in a floor joist somewhere helps; especially when working close to the edge of the stone walls. Having the roof framed in, we were ready to begin covering our structure before the winter winds began to blow.

CHAPTER TEN

FRAMING AND COVERING GABLE ENDS

Annette and I had managed to frame the roof in just a weekend. We then referred to Annette's diagrams for the gable ends and discussed the placement of the windows and vents at the peak; these all needed special framing.

Framing Details for Gable Wall with Window Opening

We began in the lower right corner of the east side gable and measured the distance from the bottom of the sill plate to the rafter directly above. This was best done with a 5' carpenter's level with an edge marking the inches. We chose to double up our 2x4 studs by nailing them together with 12ds. There are two ways that I've seen the studs cut for gable ends: overlapping the outside of the rafter with a notch in the stud end, or beveled at the top to fit snugly beneath the rafters. We chose the beveled route for the simplicity of the cut at the rafter ends.

The best way to get the angle was with a bevel and carpenter's level. We placed the adjustable metal end of the bevel underneath the rafter (just above where we took the measurement from the sill plate) making it conform to the rafter's angle and held the carpenter's level against the plastic handle of the bevel to make sure this was plumb. The measurement taken from the bottom of the sill plate to the bottom of the rafter was the length of our gable-end stud. The length of the studs will increase, obviously, as you work toward the peak of the roof. We then placed the bevel against the 2x4 studs and transferred the angle from the bevel onto them. We made the angle cuts on the 2x4s by placing them on a miter saw and lining the saw blade up to the pencil line. The other end of the stud is a straight cut. As with all framing, the studs were placed 16" apart on center, and spaced to make room for the windows and attic vent.

Framing around windows and vents is pretty easy as long as you have the correct measurements of your windows. We had the measurements for our windows, as told to us by the people who work for one of those national, chain hardware stores that are all over the country. They delivered the wrong windows four consecutive times and by the fourth time, the snow was already flying. This is the store where they drug test everyone and advertise this clearly when applying for a low-wage, service sector job. I spoke with a regional manager and after complaining more than Limbaugh out of Percocets, they sent two 5'7" trained chimps they had contracted out from Bolivia to install the WRONG windows. I called the manager back and suggested that he start administering recreational and pharmaceutical drugs to every employee in his region and described how he could probably use a quart of Jim Beam for a suppository. That was the last time we ordered anything from those Neanderthals.

Anyway, framing the windows can be done if you have the correct measurements and windows. Our larger window on the west side gable was 3-1/2'x4'. We framed up a double 2x4 stud on the right side of the window and another 3-1/2' to the left, this being the width of the window. Another 2x4 was doubled, we cut this to 3-1/2' and nailed it, lining it up to the upper mark on the vertical studs, and another 3-1/2' stud 4' below this one. A level was placed on top of the upper and lower studs and we checked them to see if they were level before driving the 16d's through them. The spaces above and below the window opening are framed as well, and the studs are spaced 16" apart, on center. Working on the studs beneath the window frame is easy since the doubled 2x4s had 2 straight cuts. We then nailed them into the lower horizontal 2x4 (also doubled) and toe nailed the bottom onto the sill plate with 16ds. The space above the window framing was a bit trickier because we had an upper beveled cut to make and then toenail the bottom to the top of the upper, horizontal 2x4.

The gable end has been covered with plywood. Wrong windows piled up.

When we framed the attic vents, we really didn't need to adjust our vertical studs since the vent was 16" wide and fit perfectly between them. So all we really needed to do was hammer the vent into the studs and add the horizontal 2x4 studs above and below the frame, nailed between the vertical studs. If you've ever asked yourself about installing attic vents, stop doing it now. They need to be installed to allow ventilation year round and they have mosquito screening on the inside to keep bugs out during the summer months.

Here, the shed dormer has been covered with plywood and tar paper.
The jack rafters have strapping on them.

With the gable ends completely framed, we rented a hydraulic scissor-lift to help install the 3/4" plywood sheathing over the studs. A strip of aluminum flashing was nailed across the sill plate to act as a water barrier between the plate and plywood sheathing. The sheathing came in 4x8 sheets, so we installed full sheets first, working our way up to the peak. The edges of the plywood met up at the center of the studs and we nailed these down as we did our floor sheathing. The edges were nailed every 6" and every 10" up and down the interior of the board, using flooring nails. When we had to cut the plywood to fit under the rafters, the angle we used was the same as the angle still set on the bevel, when we set it for the 2x4 studs. The angled cuts can be tricky, but if the bevel is set correctly it just becomes a matter of getting your pencil line straight across the board.

Since the bevel we had was only 1' long, we used carpenter's squares to get our lines straight from points a to b. A good circular saw and sharp plywood blades will zip right through the 3/4" sheets.

Annette is nailing the last piece of plywood sheathing down, the tar paper is next, then the shingles. We have some extra sand, not used for the stone walls. We covered it for the winter and used it the next year when we built the passive solar greenhouse.

We used the lift for taking the heavy sheets up and down for cutting and fitting. When the sheets were all placed and nailed down we covered the plywood with tar paper. Cutting tar paper is pretty easy with a box-cutter. We just rolled the paper out, overlapping the rafters, and then cut it down to fit underneath. A good staple gun will keep the tar paper in place and make the job quick. Tar paper is a waterproofing material that is placed between plywood sheathing and the outer covering; which was cedar shingles for us.

West side gable is ready for shingles. It was so muddy, we had to waste expensive plywood to keep the scissor-lift from sinking in and getting stuck. First floor doors and windows still need to be installed.

The stones in our house were from the driveway, and much of the wood for the framing was bought at a sawmill 3 miles down the road, as we wanted to use mainly local materials (but we didn't really obsess on it). It was just a great coincidence that there was a cedar shingle mill just down the road from us as well. The shingles were the best price we could find and were delivered without a charge. We had ordered 23 bundles, but when the delivery people saw the stone house they were curious, asked many questions and left us with 25 bundles for the price of 23. We thanked them for their generosity but they just waved us off as they were backing out of the driveway, grinning as if we'd overpaid them. They were nice people.

Annette shingling the west side of the house. We have more rows finished on the left side because moving the scaffolding and resetting it in the mud wasted too much time. The stone walls are not finished yet, they need to be "pointed", or, smoothed over on the edges with mortar to fill in the gaps and help reveal the beautiful stone faces even more.

Shingling is a simple concept, yet a tedious task to perform since there are so many of the little buggers to install, when all you really want to do is shake the frostbite from your fingertips and move into your new home. Oh well, we couldn't choose the weather, so I decided to transfer all of my anger from the numb fingertips to the seemingly endless parade of those freaking shingles. I cursed them loudly, and softly, but they still kept coming. I was thankful that they smelled nice, though, and I adapted.

We started shingling at the bottom of the plywood sheathing, moving across until the row was completed, then upward. For the first row, we took one standard shingle from the bundle and held it over the plywood, overlapping the board by 2" at the bottom. We marked the top of the shingle and did this on both sides of the gable end. With the two pencil marks on either side, we stretched a chalk line from one to the other and snapped the line. Assuming that the bottom edge of the plywood is straight and level all the way across, you shouldn't need to check the chalk line to see if it's level. It's best to slap a 5' or longer, carpenter's level on the chalk line before shingling, just to be sure that it is level, though. Even a 1/4" error from one end to the other could render that drunken, inbred hick effect on the front of your new home. Nothing quite says, "We're all from the same gene pool," like a house with screwed up shingles. It's right there when you drive up, like a six-fingered wave from the rickety porch; banjo accompaniment in the background and all.

We then lined up the tops of the shingle of the first row with the chalk line and tacked them down with (2) galvanized, 6d roofing nails. Number 2 grade shingle, the type that we bought, are usually stained or simply left to turn color naturally. The shingle mill near us had Number 1 shingles that are most often painted, and Number 4 shingles which they explained were used for under coursing, or laying 2 shingles instead of one. This is done for extra weather protection, and will cost about twice as much.

Our first course was spaced under 1/4" apart on the sides and was the only course that we doubled. The second course was lined up the same at the top and spaced over the first course so that there were no gaps. There was always one shingle covering the space made by the 2 shingles underneath, like the rule for stone laying, "one over two, two over one." Cutting the angle where the shingles meet the rafters was done by marking the side of the shingle with the bevel we had been using, still set at the same angle. We made these angle cuts with a hand jigsaw and blades for fine-cutting.

The west side gable and the dormer have been shingled. Notice the corner shingles on the dormer, the rows meet and run straight across both sides and the south face. With the shingles finished and our temporary chimney stack for our woodstove hooked up, we moved into our cozy home.

For every other course, we measured 5-1/4" up from the bottom of the previous course on the left and right sides and snapped a chalk line on the shingles. The next course was lined up with the bottom of the new shingles against the chalk line and nailed down. The sizes of our shingles varied greatly and the wider shingles needed 3 nails, about 7" up from the bottom. The nails would be covered by the following courses, overlapped by 2" of shingle.

We continued this way until we came to a course running into a window. The shingles around the windows needed to the cut short sometimes, so we drilled holes in the ends before nailing them down to prevent splitting; we placed 1x3s under the window and along the top for trim. Trying to find a shingle that is smaller than the width they usually come in is a minor problem that can be solved with a small, sharp hatchet. If we needed a 4" shingle or maybe smaller, we'd simply take the hatchet and pop the thin part of the shingle at the top, and they'd split along the grain.

When we reached the peak, the cuts became trickier and many shingles tended to break apart if we were trying to cut them too small. When we reached the peak the shingles needed angled cuts on both sides. I placed a piece of paper over the area marking the pattern that the shingle would cover and cut the paper with a box-cutter. I handed this paper pattern down to Annette: she traced it over a shingle and cut it for me. The nails at the top should be galvanized especially, since they may be exposed.

The shingling around the shed dormer provided some odd angles to work with. The east and west sides of the dormer first needed aluminum flashing tacked down along the seam between the roof and the bottom of the dormer. I folded a 10" wide aluminum strip in half lengthwise and fit the edge of the flashing into the seam. This was tacked down to the tar-papered plywood sheathing with shingling nails. The other half was screwed down to the metal roof with roofing screws and the seam between the flashing and roof was filled with a bead of tar using a tar tube and caulking gun.

Still working on the shingles for the sides of the dormer. The angled cuts
on the bottom can be tricky. They are nailed over the flashing.

After the flashing was in we could shingle the rest
without stopping, except for odd-angled cutting. Annette
doesn't mind the odd angled cutting. She can break 2 or 3
shingle without even flinching or exhibiting any eye-
twitching. Not me. After two attempts in the cold, windy
weather, I immediately started to flinch and made with the
eye tics. If the third attempt should fail, I'd have to torch
the rest of the bundle, run into the woods screaming and
drive my head into a broad oak tree. But Annette doesn't
do things like this, which is why she handled the detailed,
odd-angled cutting.

The shingles in the corners of the dormer were installed
by overlapping one edge 1/4" and meeting the other edge of
the shingle up to this. We also carried the chalk line over

from the east/west sides to the long south face. By doing this, the shingles will be even from side to side, all around the dormer.

Finishing the shingles was perhaps my favorite part of shingling. As you can see from the photos, the roof was finished before we actually finished the shingles, so this would be a convenient time to discuss how we installed the roof.

Chapter Eleven

Roofing with Steel Sheets

As you can see from the photos, we used corrugated, steel-sheet roofing to cover our rafters. Steel-sheet roofing is quite popular in the beautiful state of Maine for obvious reasons: it is extremely durable, it's lightweight, which is a plus due to the heavy snow loads, it requires minimal maintenance when installed properly, snow slides off easily, it's a fairly easy project for a do-it-yourself type, and the most important reason is the price. Steel-sheet roofing is a great bargain when considering that it will outlast regular shingles by many years.

Most stores carrying steel sheet roofing materials should have more than one type to choose from; if a particular type is not in stock, they can usually order it for you. Up here in Maine there's a religious sect that supplies steel-sheet roofing in whatever length you ask for at a real reasonable price. Unfortunately, I discovered them after my roof was installed, but the price that we paid was still reasonable for a roof. The plain, galvanized corrugated roofing was the best price for us and they came in three different lengths: 8', 10' and 12' sheets. Since we had just under 18' to cover (the length of the rafters plus some overlapping), we bought the 10' sheets.

There are a few styles to choose from when considering steel-sheet roofing. Unlike the wavy-styled corrugated, some sheets have ribs every foot or so, and when installing them the ribs on the end are actually locking channels that line up the sheets. The non-corrugated sheets are usually colored. They have a baked on enamel coating and are rather attractive when compared to the same ol', same ol' asphalt shingles that are most often gray or black. Annette and I installed a red, steel-sheet roof on an apartment building of ours and with the proper trim on the house, it really is a good-looking roof.

If you've never installed a steel-sheet roof, then you're probably asking what those thin, wooden strips running perpendicular to the rafters are. They're known as strapping, and come in a few different sizes. We bought the 1x3, pine strapping boards because they were the cheapest at the local sawmill. Roofers have used 1x4s and even 1x2s as strapping for metal roofs. Some sawmills carry the strapping boards cheap; while the big hardware stores may have the availability, you're going to pay more with them.

We nailed down our strapping with 8d nails, and spaced them 2' apart horizontally, all the way up to the peak. The ends of the strapping, where two ends meet, share ½ of the rafter when nailing them down. When spacing the strapping, we stretched a tape measure along the edge of a rafter and marked off the 2' intervals on both sides of the rafters, not on the top edge. Having the marks on the sides of the rafters allowed us to still see them when covered by the strapping. We could align the center of the board to the exact 2' mark without second guessing. At the peak, we nailed strapping down on both sides to provide a screw down surface for the ridge cap.

Working with steel sheets requires some standard safety equipment such as thick gloves for carrying sheets or touching edges, good goggles covering the entire eye area to block the fiery red bits of shrapnel flying everywhere, and ear protection. The only other sound as nasty and irritating as sawing through steel sheets could be the applause at Bush's second inauguration. I'm serious; it's really that bad, so cover those ears. Sawhorses should be used to cut the sheets on at a safe working height for the back, and if it's possible, long sleeves and thick jeans, again for the shrapnel. If a sheet should slip from your hands, you wouldn't want to be wearing Birkenstocks should it find your toes. Thick, steel-toed boots should always be worn around construction sites, anyway. Also, helpers should not stand under a sheet being raised. On one of the roofs Annette and I were working on we were careful to make sure she was out of the way before I raised the sheet upward, and we were lucky that we were being safe. The sheet slipped from my gloves, dropped around 15' or so and the edge embedded itself into a 2x4, nearly cutting it in pieces. Above all else, be patient and safe when steel roofing.

When we were cutting and installing the sheets, 2 electrical sources were needed for the circular saw and drill as well as a 100' heavy duty extension cord to go up and over the roof. The battery packs on the cordless drills run out. If you only have one then you need to wait until the thing is charged back up. Even having two drills using one as a back up, we still drained all the power out of both before the first one was even close to being charged up again. Then we were unable to finish the job that day. The cords may tend to get in the way at times but at least you know there'll be power when you need it.

Through experience, Annette and I have settled upon using a plywood-cutting circular saw blade, installed backward in the saw for cutting the steel sheets. I probably went through a half-dozen or more of those diamond composite blades before hitting on this method. The diamond blades work great, but they get eaten up by the steel and tend to shrink after each cut. A 7-1/4" blade will be the size of an Oreo after cutting through 10 or so sheets. This generally meant that we needed to stop production and change the blades frequently, wasting much time and money. The steel plywood blade should be frequently lubricated with WD-40 or something like it to make cutting easier and to extend the life of the blade. Another tip is to label this blade when you are finished roofing so that you don't inadvertently reuse it later to attempt to trim, say, an expensive door. You will be greatly disappointed if you do this, as were we.

Installing Roof Panels

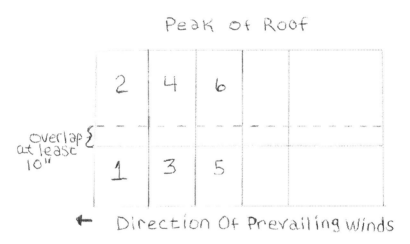

The north side of the roof had no special angles or cuts to make like the south side dormer. So, the north side was fairly simple to install, by using 10' sheets and no cuts until the ends. We installed the first sheet in the lower left corner of the roof. One thing to consider when installing a steel roof is where the prevailing winds come from. Looking at the north side of our roof, we determined that the winds would be hitting it from the right side, so the sheets to the right would overlap the sheets on the left. Starting in the lower left, we could overlap this sheet with the sheet going up to the peak, and by the sheet to the right. Vertical sheets should also overlap by 8" or more , and the overlap needs to be within 8" of a piece of strapping. If a new row of strapping is needed to meet up at the overlap, it's best to just nail down a whole row, straight across the rafters. At the bottom edge of the sheets we left a 1" overhang, and did this on the side edges as well.

Installing a 10' sheet alone can be a test of one's patience unless other methods are devised to take the place of a second person holding the sheet. I used a set of Vice Grips to clip onto the edge of a sheet, holding it tightly, and cut a 2' piece of 12 gauge insulated wire. One end of the wire was coiled around the tightening nut of the vice grips and I made a loop with the rest and wrapped the other end around the tightening nut as well. This way the wire made a handle for the Vice Grips and I could carry a sheet by holding the wire loop. This comes in handy when you're carrying a 10' sheet up the strapping, using strapping for a hand hold, and you need the second hand for climbing. When the sheet was lined up and ready to be screwed down, I put a small nail into a rafter and looped the wire around it. The Vice Grips held the sheet in place and I could use both hands for the drill and screws.

The screws used for steel sheet roofing can be bought from the same supplier that the sheets came from. The roofing screws are unique; they have a rubber gasket and a cone shaped metal covering that slightly compresses the gasket when screwed in. The two combined, they keep water out of the hole in the sheet that the screw just made. They also come in the same colors as the sheets to help avoid detection. These can be purchased in 5, 10, or 20 pound bags, and are the best fasteners to keep the steel sheets on the strapping. Two roofing companies were called for information on the latest fasteners and both recommended these screws. I never considered hiring a company of roofers, but they can be a good source of information for such things;

like the fact that neoprene nails had less success since they eventually became loose after too much ice or snow hits them.

We needed a variable speed hand drill and some special hex sockets for the screws. Buy a well-made drill for roofing because accidents happen. We also bought 6 sockets for the screws. The sockets eventually gather metal filings on the little magnet inside and it you're not careful, like me sometimes, these filings get wedged into the sides of the magnet and throw off the proper seating of the screw. The screw will spin out of synch and it becomes impossible to get through the steel. And, sometimes if the drill is held too close to the drill's tightening mechanism, the socket slips out and inevitably disappears until some string theorist calculates its whereabouts. Don't even try to find those little creeps once they're dropped. I'm pretty sure that they're each equipped with a self-losing device, ensuring that you have to buy more.

A good carpenter's apron with big pockets on the front will help carry a fair load of screws, sockets, and all the necessary roofing equipment. Annette worked on the ground cutting the sheets, handing them up to me on the roof and helping align them (making sure the bottom edges were even) by watching from off to one side. It's pretty tough trying to line up the sheets alone with only a top view of the bottom edge.

The strapping was used to climb on the roof and as a sitting place when lining up the sheets and screwing them down, so I didn't need ladder hooks or even ladders. I'd grab the sheets from Annette and lock the Vice Grips onto the edge of a long end. Then I could carry the sheet up the strapping using the wire loop for a handle and set the sheets in place.

The corrugated steel that we used was convenient when screwing the edges down. Since they are continuously wavy, the edges could be overlapped by 2 or 3 ribs to really keep the water out. I knew that overlapping with 2 ribs was sufficient but we both wanted to be absolutely certain that our roof wouldn't leak. When the long edges of the sheets were screwed down, the screws were set 1-2" from the edge of the overlapping sheet (on the right), making the edges of the top sheet snug with the bottom sheet. Each sheet was screwed down with 3 screws, spaced evenly and running horizontally, into the strapping. This was continued up to the peak; wherever a section of sheet covered strapping, 3 screws were used.

Our roof was slightly off square. So, on the west side of the roof (not the side with the main entrance) we needed to stretch a chalk line vertically up the outside edge of the sheet and make an even cut. This way the sheet edge would line up parallel to the rafter edge and not appear visibly off. We did this to the very last 2 sheets installed because steel sheets are perfectly square and won't sit correctly on a roof that isn't. The last sheets will naturally reveal the effect of the roof frame being out of square, provided that the first sheets and each thereafter were lined up as square as possible with the first rafter. So, we adjusted the last two sheets with a circular saw, cutting them parallel to the edge of the rafter leaving a 1" overhang for the trim boards to be installed just beneath.

Leaving a 1" overhang on both sides allows for room for trim boards to be nailed over the outside rafters and set under the overhang. Our rafters were 2x8s, so 1x8 trim boards were cut to the same angles as the rafters and nailed down. At the peak, the trim boards were cut to cover the ridge board as well. The two trim boards on the north and south rafters met at the center of the ridge board.

With ice, snow, and potentially hot weather affecting the roof throughout the year, it needs to be well-ventilated. In winter, the ventilation prevents ice dams from building up on the eaves. In the hot summer months an unvented roof can cause uncomfortable temperatures and higher energy bills trying to cool the house, as well as excessive humidity which can rot your framing members. Along with our two attic vents, the undersides of the rafter eaves are covered with a 1x8 soffit board. Between each rafter there's a 4"x6" hole cut into the soffit board for ventilation as well. We then cut pieces of mosquito screen big enough to cover the holes and secured them on the inside with a staple gun. This gave us decent ventilation at the eaves of the roof and combined with the ventilation at the peak, the roof was all set.

I needed now to get the ridge cap on the peak of the house and shoot some liquid dinosaur, or tar from the tar tubes, into any gaps or holes made from screws that missed the strapping beneath. With the roof in place, the best way for me to make repairs and move about afterward was to break out some ladder hooks with a 40' ladder taken apart, so that each section had a ladder hook. These were draped over the peak of the roof and they allowed me to reach anywhere on the new surface. A nice feature since the strapping can be easy to miss with the screws, and I had missed a few. Best thing to do with the screws that didn't hit the strapping was to leave them in and apply a small amount of tar around them.

The bottom edges of the east and west sides of the dormer still needed to be secured and waterproofed. We'd already placed a strip of flashing under the shingles of the dormer and left the bottom half of it sticking up. The roof sections meeting up with the bottom of the dormer were left unscrewed so the flashing could fold over this without any rips or bulges from the screws popping through. A piece of steel roof was cut lengthwise, only three ribs, so that we had an 8' piece of roof approximately 5" wide. This was placed over the flashing, covering about 2" of the edge and then screwed down into the strapping, ultimately making a flashing sandwich. The edges of the 8' piece of flashing were then sealed off with a bead of tar. After the first heavy rain in the spring, we had 2 leaks from screws that missed the scrapping and had eluded the tar as well.

We didn't have time to build the chimney so we didn't make adjustments in the roof until the next year. And, although we built the chimney the next spring, we don't use it anymore. We bought an outdoor wood-furnace that eliminated the need for a chimney. I'll describe how we built the chimney in the next chapter, but first just a couple of comments about the outdoor wood-furnaces. They're awesome. There's absolutely no chance of a fire in the house or chimney, and there's no related smoke that goes with an indoor fire. We bought our stove 2 years ago and our lives have been so much better.

We never gave the thought of burning oil any legitimacy. Oil is polluting our planet and choking the kids in our state. Seriously, kids in Maine have the highest rates of asthma in the country due to oil and coal pollution blowing our way from the rest of the nation. We chose to burn wood only for the health problems in our state and mainly because our nation is addicted to oil; a toxic slime that's killing all of us. If you live in a cold area where heat is needed and wood is plentiful (or raise your own woodlot which is what we've begun), please look into the outdoor wood-furnaces. I made this easier by including names of companies and information on how to reach them.

They are more expensive than an oil furnace initially, but with the Republicans bending over gratefully for the oil companies, the oil prices are bound to go up and stay up. If you're in the process of planning your house after reading this, than heating should be a priority. If you do choose the outdoor wood-furnace route, then like us you'll never have to worry about a chimney fire or loading dirty, sometimes bug-infested wood into your home. So now our chimney is nothing more than a right wing talk show host --unsightly and absolutely useless.

Chapter Twelve

Building the Chimney

Our chimney was built the year before we had discovered the new, outdoor stoves and we had planned on it being in the middle of the house. Chimneys need to extend 2' above the roof ridge and building it further from the ridge means extra planning. If you don't have heavy snow loads and can make do with a flat or shed style roof, than the chimney should extend over the roof by 3'. When the chimney is further from the ridge, it still needs to be built high enough to extend 2' above the ridge. This means there will be more exposure to the elements which leads to extra creosote build up and extra cleaning of the flue. Also, a chimney extending 6' or more above the roof surface will need to be supported with braces bolted into the roof surface or rafters.

We built the foundation with a pier footing in the center of the house. A chimney can weigh over a ton and should not be built without adequate ground support. Our chimney is built with (45) 16"x20" concrete chimney blocks that weigh approximately 50 pounds each. Without the mortar or flue tiles added in, the blocks alone weigh over 2,200 pounds.

To build the chimney we needed, as mentioned, 45 chimney blocks, 17 or so flue tiles, refractory cement,

cement, fine sand, hand trowels, 5 gallon buckets to haul cement inside the house, a wheelbarrow for mixing since we're not mixing too much at once, 1 steel cleanout door, a carpenter's level and a rented cement cutter.

Chimney blocks come in 2 sizes. The smaller can house 1 flue tile while the larger ones which were what we used, can hold 2. The larger ones were available at the time so we went with those. Many city codes require different flues for different heating sources so that a propane or natural gas furnace will not vent through the same flue as the wood or coal stove. The problem that could arise with having a heating unit above another within the same flue is fumes. They could be sucked into the higher placed furnace and into the home. Going with the larger concrete blocks also makes finishing the job quicker than laying regular bricks and is much cheaper.

The blocks are easy to stack and we used a mix of cement and fine sand in a 1: 9 ratio then spread this between them. There are a couple of ways to get the blocks assembled plumb. One way is to use strings with a couple of washers tied on the end and hang these just above the corners of the concrete blocks. The blocks are then placed "towing the line" as it were all the way to the roof. We use a carpenter's level placed on top and along the sides to keep them in line.

We began in the basement with a level surface and spread about 1/2" of mortar mix on the basement pad for the first block. This block was checked to make sure it was level, and then we laid 2 more down before setting in the first flue tile.

The red-clay flue tiles are 2' in length and require a substance known as refractory cement applied to the top and bottom. Just a thin layer along the edges will keep them together. Always smooth the refractory cement around the joints; don't leave any jagged spikes of cement sticking out as they can catch and build up creosote and condensation, which could affect the draw of the chimney. These tiles sit inside the chimney blocks and collect all the fumes from the heating sources. The first one we set needed a square or rectangular hole in one side, at the bottom. This is for the cleanout hole and is used as an access when getting the dried, scraped off creosote out after cleaning.

To cut the holes we used a circular saw with a cement cutting blade for the flue tiles and a power cutter for the chimney blocks. When cutting either, try to do as much outside as possible, and cutting should never be done indoors without proper ventilation. Also the power cutter is extremely loud and amazingly bad for the nose, lungs, eyes, ears, and throat, so definitely wear a respirator that works along with the usual safety equipment.

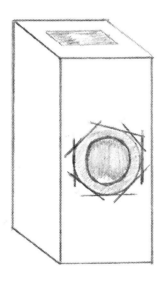

Cutting Pattern For Flue Tile

The chimney blocks needed to be cut first for the cleanout door. This was a simple rectangular cut and was done pretty quickly with the power cutter. The back of the cleanout door, the part to be cemented into the rectangular cut, was traced around the edges with a Sharpie first, right on the blocks. With the outline on the blocks, the cut was 4 straight lines and the rectangular piece of cement came out easily. A flue tile was placed inside; a hole was traced to match up with the hole in the block, and then removed for cutting.

With the cleanout holes cut in both the block and the tile, we mortared the first tile in place. We could now build up to the next flue vent hole to be cut. The "thimbles" used in the vent holes are the round, metal pieces that mount inside the block and flue tile. Other metal transition pieces can be fitted inside the thimble and they are then connected to the furnace or stove. Round holes are difficult to cut in flue tiles and one can easily end up with a broken tile. We decided to buy 3 extra flue tiles in case we broke that many.

I quickly broke the first one. I'd seen people cut these and having extras is usually something even professionals do. The hole for the thimble was traced and we cut an octagonal opening just slightly bigger than the hole we traced. The thimble fit, not as snug as I hoped, but the small spaces around the thimble were each filled with refractory cement.

Trying to cut an octagonal hole in the cement block was not even attempted due to its thickness, so we cut a square just slightly bigger than the thimble's circumference. We filled the spaces around the opening with the mortar mix then smoothed them over. We continued to lay concrete blocks and tile, making sure they were plumb until we reached the roof rafters. We had the rafters cut and supported for the chimney opening already. This was done when we set the rafters in. Now we needed to cut a hole in the steel roofing before we could place a block in the chimney opening.

Annette was inside just below the roof and I sat on the roof listening to her tap the steel with a screwdriver. I heard the tapping and sank the metal cutting blade on the circular saw into the middle of the hole and cut until I hit the wood of the rafter supports. Once I found the perimeter of the opening it was easy to cut it out. We then loaded 3 cement blocks up through the opening and onto the roof. Annette handed me a bucket with mortar, a trowel, some refractory cement, the last flue tile and a roll of lead about 8" wide.

I cemented the second to last block in place, placed more cement mix on top and folded the roll of lead over this. The idea is to drape the lead over the opening in the roof to keep the water out. I cut the lead with simple tin snips and folded a piece on each side of the block so half was lying in the concrete and the other half over the roof opening, covering it completely. Due to the angle of the roof, some pieces of lead needed to be cut longer than others. I then smoothed another layer of mortar over the lead on the block and set another block on top of this making a delicious but deadly lead sandwich. The lead is cemented between the blocks and folded downward. I screwed this down into the roof and rafters with roofing screws and squeezed a bead of tar over the edges where the lead met the roof. The last flue tile was set in before I put the last chimney block in. It was easier for me to reach the joint of the two tiles and smooth the refractory cement without the last chimney block in the way. The trick then was to lift the last chimney block over the top of the last flue tile without jarring it out of joint.

We never finished the chimney with a brick covering and I'm glad that we didn't. I may start dismantling the chimney soon since we don't need it anymore. We'll never burn oil or natural gas and the chances are slim that I'll start another fire in my house using the woodstove in the basement. Wood stoves are high maintenance and difficult to keep at a certain temperature. Keeping the house up to temperature in the winter is easier though with plenty of insulation. A penny spent now on insulation is, oh, I don't know how many in the future, but I know it's quite a bit. Speaking of insulation, the next chapter briefly covers this.

Covering Chimney Opening With Lead Flashing

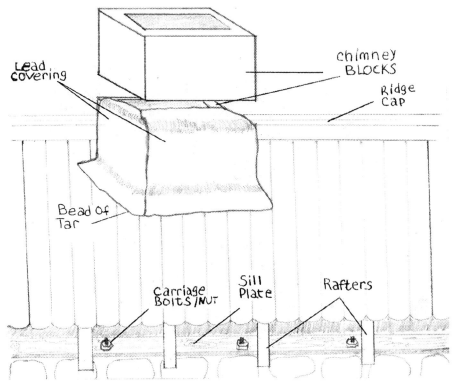

CHAPTER THIRTEEN

INSULATING OUR HOUSE

We used four types of insulation in our house. We talked about the wall insulation previously without really getting into the details. That will be done momentarily. The other two types of insulation that we installed were for the attic and between floors and they'll be discussed in order.

Our first floor walls were the first to be insulated and we used two different types. Insulation usually comes in four types: loose fill, batts, rolls, and rigid foam boards. The R-values are what to look for, the higher the R-value, the more insulating potential the product has. The U.S. Department of Energy recommends different R-values for different zones of the country. The appendix at the end includes the web site for the D.O.E.; you can find which zone you live in and insulate accordingly.

In Maine, we are considered to be zone one requiring more insulation than the other zones. Following the D.O.E. recommendations for insulating walls, we would need to have an R-value of at least 11; which just so happens to be the recommended value for every zone of the country. To meet this value, a wood framed home should use a combination of batts (pink fiberglass pre-cut into 8' lengths) and foam board. Having walls made of 1' of concrete and stone, a stone house with the standard batts which have an R-19 value will be plenty warm. We actually rolled a layer of Reflectix insulation against the stone walls and stapled them to the furring strips. This type of insulation looks like bubble packaging sandwiched by two thin layers of plastic coated aluminum foil. It can be bought in 4' wide rolls that are 25' long or 2' wide rolls that, I believe, still come in 25' long rolls and 16' long rolls. This material actually reflects cold away, if installed between the wall studs and the walls. It also reflects heat back inside the house when installed on the interior sides of the 2x4 studs. We used two layers of this, one outside and one inside of the R-19 batts, between the studs.

In all, our walls are 1' thick with concrete and stone, a layer of Reflectix against the walls, a ¼" air space between the R-19 and the first layer, a second layer of Reflectix on the inside of the wall studs, a layer of ½" drywall and all this is covered by 1 x 8, v-notch pine boards. The combined width of the walls is just less than 18", providing a warm, snug environment inside. With wood framed walls, it may be best to take the D.O.E.'s suggestion and use 2x6 studs. Doing this increases the space for insulation such as a layer of foam board, having an R-value of 4 -7 and rolling the R-19 batts between the studs for an R-value exceeding 20. We chose to use the standard 2x4's and plenty of pink, fiberglass insulation in our dormer.

The wood framed walls of our shed dormer were not as thick as the first floor, obviously, so we used R-39, attic blanket cut to fit between the wall studs. Since there is an air space between the walls of the shed dormer and the interior walls, we figured that it would be best to pack in the thick stuff.

For attic areas, the D.O.E. recommends an R-value of 49 for houses in zone 1, 38 for zones 2-4, 30 for zones 3-7 and an R-19 value for zone 8, which includes the southernmost tips of Florida, Texas and California. We bought bundles of attic blanket to cover the attic floor. We first set down a layer of R-19 in rolls, not batts, covering every inch of the attic floor right up to the rafters. On top of the R-19, we placed the attic blanket. The attic blanket came in bundles of compressed 3'x3' or 3'x4' rectangular pieces, and can be placed side by side, corner to corner when filling the attic floor. Using two layers of attic blanket in the coldest areas would help lower energy costs, whether the house is made of stone or not.

In every part of the country, the D.O.E. recommends insulation with an R-value of at least 19 for floors over unheated crawl spaces or basements. This is easily done by using the R-19 rolls and a staple gun. Between the 2x10 joists, roll out the insulation until the blockers are in the way and cut it there, then continue on the other side until the entire gap is filled. The paper on the insulation has folds that can be unfolded to help staple it to the joists. Annette and I didn't install R-19 between our floor joists because we had planned on installing plastic pex tubing for radiant floor heating.

The next summer we were able buy the outdoor woodstove I've raved about already, and we installed the radiant heat tubing between the joists. The tubing is held against the bottom of the plywood flooring with aluminum flashing and 12mm staples. We then rolled some more Reflectix over the tubing and flashing, between the joists, to keep the heat from going anywhere but toward the floor. The tubing carries hot water from the stove with the help of a circulator pump. There isn't a cold spot to step on all winter, and it's funny to watch the pets flatten themselves out across the floor sucking up the heat.

In the winter of 2004, we bought 10 cords of tree length logs for fuel at $45 per cord. For $450, we had heat and enough hot water to bathe a woolly mammoth every day for the whole winter. We needed to take a chainsaw to the logs and stack the wood, ourselves. But, when I consider the fact that I'm working for our heat and not working for someone else, having to earn the cash to then turn around and hand it to the oil companies for their filthy "Texas Tea" to heat our home and poison the beautiful surroundings, I'll wield the chainsaw better than that maniac from Texas any day. The trees on our property are still pretty thin from the logging goons clear-cutting everything seven years ago. In a few more years we should be cutting and using our own firewood, thus eliminating the callous oil conglomerates, their Saudi buddies and even the bill for wood deliveries. Heating oil is over $2 per gallon as I'm writing this, and with the New World Order gang controlling the energy supply to our country, we can expect to see more and more individual incomes being collected by the oil companies who exhibit zero respect for the toil and sweat of workers, or the environment.

We've planned on eliminating our electricity costs in the next year or two, with wind and solar collectors. The prices are still pretty steep to outfit an entire house with alternative energy sources, but I'm counting on more advances coming out of backyard, American tool sheds, and basements; from the Edisonesque genius inherent in all Americans when our backs are to the wall. Battery storage and inverter units to transfer the battery D.C. power to home A.C. current will be as cheap to buy as a video game system soon enough, and we'll be producing our own power. We need to get away from the economic controls forced upon us by the climbing costs of fuel. Fuel is running our lives. Stop and think about how much you spent on oil last year to heat your home. At your current rate of pay, calculate how many hours you had to work for someone else, to foot the oil bill for one year. As Americans, being dependent on oil and having to work extra to keep up with the rising costs, is simply a form of control and enslavement.

Since Bush stole the Florida election and the country in 2000, the oil companies have been frothing at the mouth. Controlling the energy supply does many things to helpless Americans; namely, increasing the amount of work one needs to do to afford the same, basic necessities. This situation often mandates that there be extra income earners in the same household, which means that both parents need to leave the home to earn money. This leaves the American kids with less parental support and guidance, creating the potential for juvenile delinquency and unusual stresses on the family. I know. I've seen this happening with my own eyes, while working as a social worker in Maine. Remember the "family values" that King George II lied so much about? Well, the compassionate neo-conmen have decided that making money and destroying our environment is much more important than we are. As Americans, it's time to stand and collectively scream, "F&#@ YOU," to all corporate controls.

Avoid the controls of bank enslavement by not purchasing an outrageously priced house on the market. Don't feed the corporate beasts by buying overpriced wood and other basic building items. Home Depot donated a sickening amount to the Bush thugs in the 2004 façade, I mean election. They'll never get another penny of mine if I can help it. Build your own house with the cheapest and best material in the world, stone, and avoid the system as much as possible. For Annette and I, building our own stone house was as much an act of subversion as it was necessity. Whenever I thought of shaking the cold, manicured hands of some whimpy banker, signing the next 30 years of my life away to support his right wing lifestyle, I damn near puked my toes up. That's not what I consider helping ourselves to a slice of the American pie. It's more like having the pie dangled in front of you until your body is too broken and the mind to weak to finally enjoy it. So, for yourself, the environment and your kids, build a stone house; then you can take infinite solace in the fact that you've done not only the right thing, but possibly the coolest thing you will ever do.

When I was younger, I thought skiing on acid was the coolest thing ever; not even close. There are incredible feelings of self-satisfaction and pride that hit me every time I look at our home. When coming home in the dark, wintery nights, it's awful comforting to set my eyes on the stone structure, knowing how warm and cozy it is inside. And I swear to Jerry, that last summer I actually caught myself hugging the southwest corner. Annette and I will both openly admit that neither of us are poets, musicians, or artists in any way. And yet, we both feel that we've finally painted our masterpiece.

Total Costs

WOOD FOR FORMS

1 x 6 unplaned spruce (750 ft. @ .20 psf)
$150.00

2 x 4 x 8's (180 @ 1.89)
$340.20

TOOLS AND EQUIPMENT

Circular saw
$125.00

Miter saw
$109.00

Jig saw
$ 79.00

Hand tools
$100.00

Used cement mixer
$ 75.00

Wheelbarrow
$ 69.00

Shovels
$ 40.00

Excavation (With Basement)
$500.00

CEMENT

Footing
$1140.00

Basement walls
$1600.00

Pier footings
$130.00

Stone/cement walls (80 bags   @7.00)
$560.0

Gravel (screened for cement, 10 yards @ 6.75)
$ 67.50

Sand (12 yards @ 6.75)
$ 81.00

Rebar
$700.00

Wire (#9 gauge, 50 lb.) x 2
$ 90.00

WOOD

Girders
$145.00

Joists: 1st and 2nd floors(97- 2x10x14)
$1174.00

Studs (155- 2x4x8)
$349.00

Stair carriages (7 -2x12x16)
$105,00

Rafters (38- 2x8x20)
$587.00

Dormer rafters (20 -2x8x14)
$165.00

Gable end (24- 2x4x12)
$ 78.72

Gable end (24- 2x6x12)
$116.40

Plywood sub-floor: 1st and 2nd floors
(81 -23/32, 4 x 8 fir)
$1899.00

Ridge board (2- 2 x 10 x20)
$ 33.80

Strapping: 1 x 3 x 8, planed spruce (90 @ .95)
$ 85.50

Door/window frame (18- 2 x 10 x12)
$175.00

Cedar shingles
$355.00

Corrugated Roofing
$466.00

Ridge cap
$ 30.00

Joist hangers
$ 45.00

Lolly columns
$ 66.00

Nails, screws, bolts
$350.00

Miscellaneous expenses
$3000.00

Total
$15,181.12

COMPANIES TO CHECK OUT

Bioshield: an environmentally friendly paint company.
Contact them at:
www.bioshieldpaint.com, or toll free at 1-800-621-2591.

Wood Doctor Outdoor Hotwater Wood Furnaces: possibly
the best way to heat your home. P.O. Box 567, Stewiacke,
Nova Scotia B0N 2J0. (902)-639-9171.

REFERENCES

Schwenke, Karl, Build Your Own Stone House: Using The Easy Slipform Method ,

2nd Edition, Pownal, Vermont: Storey Pub. Co., 1991.

International Building Codes 2003, published by the International Codes Council,

Country Club Hills, Illinois, 2002.

Nash, George, Do It Yourself Homebuilding: The Complete Handbook, New York:

Sterling Publishing Company, 1995.

Reader's Digest Books, Back To Basics. How to Learn and Enjoy Traditional American Skills

The Reader's Digest Association, Inc. Pleasantville, New York/Montreal.

Department of Energy's website for insulation/R-value information: www.eere.energy.gov.

Nearing, Helen and Scot. <u>Living the Good Life.</u> New York; Shocken, 1970.

Printed in the United States
66496LVS00006B/62

9 781595 260208